CLASS

The *Friendly* Guide to

Beethoven

CLASSIC *f*M

The *Friendly* Guide to

Beethoven

John Suchet
and Darren Henley

Hodder Arnold

www.hoddereducation.com

For UK order enquiries: please contact Bookpoint Ltd, 130 Milton Park, Abingdon, Oxon OX14 4SB. Telephone: +44(0) 1235 827720. Fax: +44(0) 1235 400454. Lines are open 09.00–18.00, Monday to Saturday, with a 24-hour message answering service. You can also order through our website www.hoddereducation.com

British Library Cataloguing in Publication Data: a catalogue record for this title is available from the British Library.

First published in UK 2006, by Hodder Education, 338 Euston Road, London NW1 3BH.

Typeset by Servis Filmsetting Ltd, Manchester
Printed in Great Britain for Hodder Education, a division of Hodder Headline, 338 Euston Road, London NW1 3BH, by Cox & Wyman Ltd, Reading, Berkshire.

Hodder Headline's policy is to use papers that are natural, renewable and recyclable products and made from wood grown in sustainable forests. The logging and manufacturing processes are expected to conform to the environmental regulations of the country of origin.

Impression number   10 9 8 7 6 5 4 3 2 1

Year   2010 2009 2008 2007 2006

"From the heart — may it return to the heart."
Ludwig van Beethoven

"The Last Master of resounding song, the tuneful heir of Bach and Handel, Mozart and Haydn's immortal fame, is no more. The harp is hushed. He was an artist, and who shall arise to stand beside him? He was an artist. Thus he was, thus he died, and thus he will live until the end of time."
Franz Grillparzer, the Funeral Oration

 contents

Contents

A Friendly Word Before We Get Started . . .

This is the second book in our series of Classic FM Friendly Guides. Following the success of *The Classic FM Friendly Guide to Mozart*, we decided to turn our attention to his great rival for the title of the world's favourite classical composer – Ludwig van Beethoven.

On the Classic FM team, we are lucky enough to have a real Beethoven specialist in the form of John Suchet and we are delighted that, after a very long and expensive lunch, he was persuaded to share his

insight into the great man's life and music in this book.

Everything that you read over the next 200 or so pages remains true to our mission at Classic FM to break down the barriers that have sometimes surrounded classical music over the years.

We established two rules about how pieces of music would appear in our Mozart book. There is no reason that what worked well for Mozart won't be equally as good for Beethoven, so:

- Titles of musical works are set in italics.
- Songs appear in italics within quotation marks.

Most of Beethoven's works were given a catalogue or "Opus" number. We have included these in the titles of works where more than one piece has the same name, or no name. That will help you to track it down, should you want to investigate further. And one final note of explanation: some of Beethoven's music was not catalogued and these pieces are given a "WoO No." ("without Opus number").

Darren Henley
Station Manager
Classic FM

x

Introduction

Who is the greatest composer of them all, Mozart
or Beethoven? The argument has raged for years,
decades, more than a century, in fact.

The last half of the 19th century belonged to
Beethoven, as fellow greats such as Brahms, Wagner,
Bruckner, Mahler, all declared their debt to him. In
the first half of the last century Mozart held the
ascendancy. World War Two, with the opening beats
of the *Fifth Symphony* broadcast by the BBC to the
Free French, put Beethoven back on top. The last
part of the 20th century, with the film *Amadeus*, the
bicentenary of his death in 1991 and more recently
the 250th anniversary of his birth in 2006, gave the
number one spot back to Mozart.

So start getting ready now for the massive commemorations to come in 2027, as the world marks the 200th anniversary of the death of Ludwig van Beethoven, and he moves once again effortlessly into the top spot. There will be millions more words in scores of new books, thousands of concerts, certainly a film or two, not to mention countless radio and television programmes.

His image will be everywhere, portraying him no doubt as some sort of god-like creature, permanently frowning, angels and cherubs at his feet, atop a marble plinth or on a sculpted column like a Roman emperor. Indeed my own bronze life mask of him – gazing at me imperiously and divinely as I write – is crowned by laurel leaves.

Let us get it straight from the start: Beethoven was not a god, and his music was not perfect. Even he acknowledged it. He once wrote to his frustrated publisher, after demanding changes to works which were about to be published:

One must not hold oneself so divine as to be unwilling occasionally to make improvements in one's creations.

All right, he may not have been a *mere* mortal, but mortal he was, with all the failings of one. He had broken love affairs, he upset friends, he drank too much, he was moody, he had a temper.

And, of course, he went deaf. That is the one thing everybody knows about Beethoven. Mind you, some people know a little more than others. I was on my way to the local theatre in Inverness to give my Beethoven talk, and the taxi driver asked me who I was giving my talk about. I replied, somewhat hesitantly, keen not to sound too serious or artistically heavyweight: "Er . . . Beethoven." "Oh aye," he said, and went quiet for a minute or two. Then, sitting behind him, it was as if I saw the light bulb go on in his head. "Beethoven. I know him. He's the one who cut his ear off."

If that makes you smile, it's a rare moment of humour in anything to do with Beethoven. We're accustomed to seeing him and his listeners in contemporary prints, their faces etched with seriousness and gravitas (in contrast to Schubert and his friends, always portrayed smiling and singing).

Much of Beethoven's music *is* serious. But approach it with an open mind, and you will also discover some of the most beautiful, lyrical, gentle music ever written. Music that will bring a smile of familiarity to your face. Why? Because if art was his god, and music its most important expression, he was using art and music not to express some vision of the ethereal, but to hold a mirror up to life itself. A young musician asked him where he got his ideas.

He answered:

That I cannot tell you with certainty. They come unsummoned, directly, indirectly. I could seize them with my hands, out in the open air, in the woods, while walking, in the silence of the nights, early in the morning; incited by moods which the poet translates into words, but which I turn into tones that sound, and roar, and storm about me until I have set them down in notes.

Mind you, he also said:

I do not write what I most desire to, but what I need to because of money.

That's Beethoven. Man of contradictions. And surely no contradiction is more inexplicable than that a composer slowly but surely losing his hearing was able to compose some of the greatest music ever written.

Since I was commissioned to write this book by Classic FM as one of a series (the lunch wasn't necessary: my reluctance was a bluff), I have asked my Classic FM colleague Darren Henley to provide the later chapters on associated issues such as movie music and quotations, and chapters directly involving Classic FM.

I am responsible for all the narrative chapters
(Chapters 1–10). Given that there are already
thousands of books available on Beethoven (with,
as I have said, many more to come), and countless
pages available on the internet, I have tried at all
times to offer something more – facts about
Beethoven and those close to him which are little
known or in some cases unknown, and which (I
hope) will make you smile or gasp in astonishment.
I know for certain that some of my revelations have
never been published before.

The result is, I believe, a book more immediate,
more accessible, easier to read, more *friendly* than
many of those that have been written about this
remarkable artist.

John Suchet
May 2006

The Friendly Guide to What Was Composed When

YEAR	What was happening to Beethoven?	What was Beethoven composing?	What else was going on in the world?
1770	Beethoven is baptized on 17 December (probably born on 16 Dec). He is his parents' second child, but the first one to survive		The French dauphin (later Louis XVI) marries the Habsburg Archduchess Marie Antoinette Captain Cook claims eastern coast of New Holland (Australia) for Great Britain Italian composer Tartini dies William Wordsworth born
1771			The first *Encyclopaedia Britannica* issued by a "Society of Gentlemen in Scotland" Plague in Moscow kills 57,000 Russia occupies Crimea in war against Turkey Sir Walter Scott born
1772			Mozart appointed *Konzertmeister* in Salzburg Haydn composes "Sturm und Drang" symphonies, nos. 43–7 First partition of Poland between Prussia and Russia

		Captain Cook's second voyage of discovery, in the *Resolution*
		Samuel Coleridge Taylor born
1773	Grandfather Ludwig dies	"Boston Tea Party" takes place
		Foundation of the Royal Swedish Opera
		Captain Cook first European explorer to cross Antarctic Circle
1774	Brother Caspar Carl is born	Antonio Salieri appointed *Kapellmeister* in Vienna
		Louis XVI becomes King of France
		First continental congress in the American colonies meets in Philadelphia and passes the Declaration of Rights
		Russia and Turkey end six-year war
1775		Mozart composes his five *Violin Concertos*
		American War of Independence begins
		George Washington appointed commander of continental army
		Jane Austen born

CONTINUED ▶

YEAR	What was happening to Beethoven?	What was Beethoven composing?	What else was going on in the world?
1776	Brother Nikolaus Johann is born		American declaration of independence on 4 July Gibbon publishes *Decline and Fall of the Roman Empire* Captain Cook embarks on third, and fatal, voyage to the Pacific Ocean E.T.A. Hoffmann, music critic who will recognize Beethoven's genius, is born
1777			Stars and Stripes adopted as flag of the US Tsar Alexander of Russia born
1778	The boy, aged 7¾, gives his first public performance, in Cologne, playing "various piano concertos and trios". On the poster his father wrongly gives his age as 6		France declares war on Great Britain and joins the American War of Independence War of Bavarian Succession between Austria and Prussia Thomas Arne, English composer, dies Philosophers Voltaire and Rousseau die
1779	Neefe arrives in Bonn and soon becomes Beethoven's first full-time teacher		First all-cast-iron bridge built across the River Severn at Ironbridge English inventor, Samuel Crompton,

			invents the spinning mule War of Bavarian Succession ends Captain Cook is killed in Hawaii
1780			Death of Empress Maria Theresa Joseph II, who has been Emperor since 1765, takes sole control of Habsburg dominions, and begins a series of wide-ranging reforms First Epsom Derby run
1781	Beethoven taken out of school by his father, who wants him to earn money for the family as a child prodigy, just as the young Mozart had done		Mozart, dismissed by the Archbishop of Salzburg, settles in Vienna Joseph II introduces religious tolerance to the Habsburg lands Sir William Herschel discovers the planet Uranus William Pitt the Younger, later Prime Minister, enters Parliament General Cornwallis surrenders at Yorktown, Virginia, ending the American Revolutionary War Kant publishes his *Critique of Pure Reason*

CONTINUED ▶

YEAR	What was happening to Beethoven?	What was Beethoven composing?	What else was going on in the world?
1782	Neefe is appointed court organist, and allows Beethoven to stand in for him to give him experience Either this year, or soon after, Beethoven gets to know the Breuning family, teaching the Breuning children piano and spending a lot of time in their sophisticated and cultured home. He also forms a friendship with Wegeler	He publishes his first composition, *Variations on a March by Dressler*	George Washington creates military medal later named "Purple Heart" Nicolo Paganini, Italian violinist and composer, born J.C. Bach dies
1783	Beethoven travels to Holland with his mother, where he performs at court in the Hague. He returns with no money, but plenty of snuff boxes and other small presents, to his father's annoyance Neefe writes in a music magazine that if Beethoven were allowed to travel, he would become a second Mozart	He publishes three *Piano Sonatas* dedicated to the Elector, known as the *Kurfürsten Sonatas*	Britain and US sign peace treaty and Britain formally recognizes American independence The Montgolfier brothers give the first demonstration of hot air balloons
1784	Maximilian Franz, brother of the Emperor, becomes Elector in Bonn, and greatly encourages Beethoven		William Pitt the Younger becomes Prime Minister at the age of 24, Britain's youngest ever Prime Minister

1785	Beethoven gets his first paid job, assistant court organist alongside Neefe, at a salary of 150 florins	He composes three *Piano Quartets*	Russia annexes control of Crimea from Turkey John Wesley establishes the Methodist Church Samuel Johnson, English writer, born Edmund Cartwright invents the power loom First crossing of English Channel by air in hydrogen gas balloon Dollar chosen as money unit for the US
1786			Mozart premieres *The Marriage of Figaro* in Vienna Goethe undertakes his "Italian Journey" Robert Burns publishes *Poems, Chiefly in the Scottish Dialect* First ship of convicts leaves for Botany Bay, Australia Mont Blanc climbed for the first time Carl Maria Weber born King Ludwig of Bavaria, Wagner's future patron, born Frederick the Great of Prussia dies

CONTINUED ▶

7

YEAR	What was happening to Beethoven?	What was Beethoven composing?	What else was going on in the world?
1787	Beethoven, aged 16, leaves his home and family for the first time and travels to Vienna to meet Mozart. He plays for him and the great man agrees to take him on as a student. But he receives word from his father that his mother is dangerously ill, and he has to leave for home without beginning lessons with Mozart. His mother dies of consumption within three months of his return		Mozart's father, Leopold Mozart, dies Mozart premieres *Don Giovanni* in Prague US Constitution is adopted, federal government is established, and Delaware becomes first US state, followed by Pennsylvania and New Jersey Christoph Willibald von Gluck dies
1788	Count Waldstein arrives in Bonn, taking Beethoven under his wing and becoming his first important patron. He will later receive dedication of the *Waldstein Sonata* in gratitude		*The Times* newspaper begins publication in London Fire destroys much of New Orleans, leaving one-quarter of the population dead First convict settlement established at Botany Bay, Australia Lord Byron, English poet, born C.P.E. Bach dies
1789	Beethoven's father is forced to retire. Henceforth one half of his 200-thaler		The French Revolution begins, with the storming of the Bastille on 14 July

	salary will be paid to Beethoven for the support of the family He gets invaluable experience of orchestration playing viola in the court orchestra		George Washington elected first President of US Fletcher Christian leads mutiny on the Bounty against Captain Bligh
1790	Beethoven receives his first important commission, when Emperor Joseph dies and is succeeded by his brother Leopold	Beethoven composes cantatas to commemorate both events, but they are not performed in public because several of the orchestral players declare them impossible to play	Mozart premieres *Così fan Tutte* in Vienna France is reorganized into *départements* Emperor Joseph dies, succeeded by his brother Leopold
1791	Beethoven goes on a boat journey to Mergentheim, to the Elector's summer palace, with the other members of the court orchestra. Being the youngest, he is appointed kitchen scullion for the voyage	He composes the *Ritterballet* for Count Waldstein, who passes it off as his own composition	Mozart premieres *The Magic Flute* in Vienna. He composes his *Clarinet Concerto* and struggles to complete his *Requiem*, but death takes him on 5 December with the *Requiem* unfinished The *Observer* newspaper begins publication in London James Boswell publishes *The Life of Samuel Johnson*
1792	A crucial year for Beethoven. Haydn passes through Bonn, meets Beethoven, and offers to take him on		Emperor Leopold dies suddenly, succeeded by Emperor Franz French monarchy is overthrown and

CONTINUED ▶

YEAR	What was happening to Beethoven?	What was Beethoven composing?	What else was going on in the world?
	as a pupil if he can make his way to Vienna With French troops occupying the Rhine area, the court orchestra is disbanded and the Elector leaves Bonn. This allows Beethoven to travel to Vienna in November, where he expects to stay for a few months. He remains there for the rest of his life In December his father dies		France is declared a republic France declares war against Austria Guillotine used for the first time in France La Marseillaise composed by Rouget de Lisle English poet Shelley born
1793	Beethoven's first full year in Vienna He takes up lessons with Haydn	"Se vuol ballare" Variations (from Mozart's Marriage of Figaro) for piano and violin published	Execution of Louis XVI (January) and Marie Antoinette (October) The allies declare war on France Napoleon Bonaparte, as Artillery Commander, has first military victory at Toulon Second partition of Poland by Russia and Prussia Paganini makes his debut, aged 11
1794	Beethoven's brother Caspar Carl moves to Vienna	Since meeting Mozart six years earlier, he has been working on a Piano	Robespierre overthrown and guillotined

	Haydn leaves for his second visit to England	*Concerto*. He now revises it and brings it to fruition. It is his first truly substantial work, although it will be published as his *Piano Concerto No. 2* He also begins work on what will become his first major publication, the *Piano Trios Op. 1*	Nelson loses sight in his right eye at the Battle of Calvi
1795	Beethoven gives his first public performance, playing his *Piano Concerto No. 2*. Later in the year he performs his *Piano Concerto No. 1*. (There's some doubt as to what order he played them in, but by the end of the year he had certainly performed both) He tries to impress his teacher by performing his *Piano Trios* before Haydn, who has the temerity to be critical He later performs his first set of *Piano Sonatas* for Haydn. Haydn obviously reacted more favourably this time, since Beethoven dedicated them to him Beethoven obviously thinks he's	He completes his second piano concerto, published as *Piano Concerto No. 1*, only two days before performing it *Piano Trios Op. 1* are published He composes his first set of three *Piano Sonatas*	France makes peace with Prussia, Holland, and Spain France annexes Austrian Netherlands and creates "Belgian departments" Napoleon appointed Commander of the Army of the Interior The *Marseillaise* officially adopted as French national anthem John Keats, English poet, is born

CONTINUED ▶

YEAR	What was happening to Beethoven?	What was Beethoven composing?	What else was going on in the world?
	"arrived", since he reportedly proposes marriage to an old friend from Bonn, Magdalena Willman. She turns him down Brother Nikolaus Johann arrives in Vienna. Both his brothers are now there, and cause Beethoven endless problems		
1796	Beethoven's first extensive concert tour. He performs in Prague, Dresden, Leipzig and Berlin	In Prague he composes *Ah! Perfido* for soprano and orchestra. In Berlin he composes a set of *Cello Sonatas* for the local virtuoso	Napoleon marries Josephine and scores brilliant victories over the Austrians in northern Italy First smallpox vaccination administered by Edward Jenner Catherine the Great of Russia dies, and is succeeded by her son Tsar Paul I
1797	Beethoven takes part in the first performance of his *Quintet Op. 16* at Jahn's restaurant He falls seriously ill, probably with typhus, and it is possible this triggered the onset of his deafness	He's now into his stride and composes several *Piano Sonatas*	Austria and France sign a peace treaty Napoleon conquers Venice, ending 1070 years of independence

		Haydn composes the music that will become the German national anthem Franz Schubert born
1798	Beethoven gives several public performances in Vienna, and prepares a number of works for publication He visits Prague for the second time and performs there	He composes the first "big one" among the *Piano Sonatas*, the *Pathétique*, as well as several other sonatas Begins work on his first *String Quartets*	Napoleon embarks on the Egyptian expedition, but Nelson destroys his fleet at the Battle of the Nile Irish nationalists, assisted by French troops, rebel against British occupation
1799	Beethoven begins studies in vocal composition with Salieri He meets the double bass virtuoso, Dragonetti, which revolutionizes his thinking about the instrument's potential	Completes his first *String Quartet* Begins work (comparatively late, since he is now 28) on *Symphony No. 1*	Napoleon becomes First Consul of France Income tax first introduced in England George Washington dies
1800	Beethoven gives his first benefit concert in Vienna, premiering his *Septet* and *Symphony No. 1* He comprehensively defeats Daniel Steibelt in an improvisation contest, establishing himself as Vienna's foremost piano virtuoso	He completes a *Violin Sonata* and a *Horn Sonata*, as well as his first set of *String Quartets* Begins work on *Septet* and *Piano Concerto No. 3* Completes *Symphony No. 1* and begins work on *Symphony No. 2*	Napoleon defeats the Austrians comprehensively at Marengo, and expels them from northern Italy Act of Union incorporates Ireland into the UK British troops expel the French from Malta Puccini, Italian composer, dies

CONTINUED ▶

YEAR	What was happening to Beethoven?	What was Beethoven composing?	What else was going on in the world?
1801	Traumatic year for Beethoven. For the first time, in a letter to an old friend, he acknowledges his deafness He falls in love with his pupil, Giulietta Guicciardi, to whom he will dedicate the *Moonlight Sonata*	Composes the *Piano Sonata Op. 27 No. 2*, which will become known as the *Moonlight Sonata* Composes other *Piano Sonatas* and *Violin Sonatas*, and the ballet *Creatures of Prometheus*	Austria and France sign another peace treaty Tsar Paul of Russia is assassinated, succeeded by his son Alexander Nelson wins the Battle of Copenhagen
1802	Another traumatic year for Beethoven. He writes the *Heiligenstadt Testament*, telling posterity that his deafness made him withdraw from mankind. He realizes now that it is incurable	Composes the *Eroica Variations*, several more *Piano Sonatas*, the *String Quintet*, and completes *Symphony No. 2*	Britain and France sign the Treaty of Amiens Napoleon confirmed as Consul for life. Victor Hugo, French author, born
1803	Beethoven is appointed composer-in-residence at the Theater an der Wien Holds a benefit concert there of his own works: *Second Symphony* and *Third Piano Concerto* are heard for the first time Performs the *Kreutzer Sonata* with the English mulatto violinist, George Bridgetower	The single most important composition to date – one that was to change the course of musical history – is written: the *Eroica Symphony*. Also composes the *Violin Sonata* that will become known as the *Kreutzer*, and the *Waldstein Piano Sonata* Big compositions, which is why this is often referred to as the beginning of Beethoven's *Heroic Period*	Napoleon abolishes the Holy Roman Empire. Soon the Holy Roman Emperor will become merely the Emperor of Austria. US buys Louisiana and New Orleans from France First public railway line in the world is opened between Wandsworth and Croydon Hector Berlioz is born

1804	Beethoven is commissioned to write an opera, but struggles with a poor libretto He first meets Josephine Brunsvik, with whom he falls in love On hearing that Napoleon has declared himself Emperor, he tears up the title page of the *Eroica Symphony*, containing the dedication to Napoleon	Begins work on the opera that, a decade later, will become *Fidelio*. Composes the *Triple Concerto*, and more piano works	Napoleon crowns himself Emperor of France Napoleonic Code adopted as French civil law William Pitt the Younger begins second term as Prime Minister Spain declares war on Britain Johann Strauss senior born Benjamin Disraeli, future Prime Minister, born
1805	First public performance of Beethoven's greatest work to date, the *Eroica Symphony* Beethoven stages his opera, *Leonore*, but the occupying French army forces it to close	Completes his opera, *Leonore*, but it will be substantially reworked. Composes the *Appassionata Piano Sonata*	French army occupies Vienna. Napoleon establishes headquarters at Schönbrunn Palace Napoleon scores one of his greatest victories at Austerlitz, but the French fleet is defeated by Nelson at Trafalgar France and Austria sign peace treaty Schiller, German playwright, dies Boccherini, Italian composer, dies
1806	Revised *Leonore* is performed, but Beethoven is still dissatisfied and withdraws it	Huge year for compositions, despite all the personal traumas. *Piano Concerto No. 4*, *Razumovsky Quartets*,	Napoleon defeats Prussia, occupies Berlin, and closes all continental ports to British ships in an attempt to cripple the economy

CONTINUED ▶

YEAR	What was happening to Beethoven?	What was Beethoven composing?	What else was going on in the world?
	Prince Lichnowsky takes Beethoven away to his country estate for some R&R. But Beethoven quarrels violently with his patron and treks home alone	*Symphony No. 4, Violin Concerto*, all composed	Holy Roman Empire officially ceases to exist William Pitt the Younger dies
1807	Beethoven writes several letters to the widowed Josephine Brunsvik, asking for a physical relationship. She rejects him Several performances of Beethoven's works during the year, with the composer himself reportedly conducting the *Eroica* on 6 December He performs his new *Mass in C* for Prince Esterhazy, but the Prince does not like it	Spends most of the year working on another "big one", the *Fifth Symphony*, no less Also composes the *Mass in C*	Napoleon and the Tsar carve up Poland. France, Prussia and Russia sign the Peace of Tilsit Slave trade abolished in the British Empire
1808	Difficult year for Beethoven. He is offered a benefit concert, which is postponed again and again In frustration he accepts an appointment as *Kapellmeister* for King	Completes the *Fifth* and *Sixth* (*Pastoral*) *Symphonies, Piano Trios* and a *Cello Sonata*	Peninsular War begins. Sir Arthur Wellesley, later the Duke of Wellington, takes on Napoleon's forces in Portugal and Spain Russian troops occupy Finland. Tsar

Year	Beethoven's life	Compositions	World events
	Jerome (Napoleon's brother) in Kassel, Westphalia, on a huge salary. Archduke Rudolph and two other aristocrats soon offer him an annuity to remain in Vienna, which he accepts. Benefit concert takes place on 22 December, and is a disaster. But for the first time, the *Fifth* and *Sixth Symphonies* are heard. It is arguably the most important concert of Beethoven's life		Alexander declares Finland a part of Russia
1809	Beethoven begins teaching piano and composition to his greatest patron, Archduke Rudolph. But the Archduke, along with the Imperial royal family, flee Vienna when the French invade. Beethoven takes refuge in his brother's cellar, holding cushions to his ears, during the bombardment. Almost unnoticed during the invasion, Haydn dies, to Beethoven's distress	Completes the *Fifth Piano Concerto* (*The Emperor*), several *Piano Sonatas* including the *Lebewohl* [*Farewell*] to mark Archduke Rudolph's departure, and a *String Quartet*	Austria declares war on France. Wellesley defeats the French in Portugal and becomes Viscount (later Duke of) Wellington. Royal Opera House opens in London. Felix Mendelssohn and Abraham Lincoln born
1810	Beethoven falls in love with another pupil, Therese Malfatti, asking	Composes incidental music for Goethe's *Egmont*, and another *String*	Chopin and Schumann both born in this year

CONTINUED ▶

YEAR	What was happening to Beethoven?	What was Beethoven composing?	What else was going on in the world?
	Wegeler to send him his baptismal certificate in preparation for marriage. He presents her with the *Bagatelle, Für Elise*. She turns him down flat	*Quartet*. Begins work on the *Archduke Trio*	Napoleon adds insult to injury, having defeated the Austrians on the battlefield more times than he can remember, by marrying the Emperor's daughter, Marie-Louise
1811	Beethoven gets to know Antonie Brentano, the strongest candidate for the "Immortal Beloved", visiting her often and playing the piano for her when she falls ill	Begins work on the *Seventh Symphony* Completes the *Archduke Trio* Composes theatre music for *King Stephen* and *The Ruins of Athens*	More French losses in Portugal and Spain Franz Liszt is born
1812	A big year. The year of the affair with the "Immortal Beloved" in Prague. In Teplitz immediately afterwards, he writes the famous "Letter to the Immortal Beloved", and meets Goethe, whose works he much admires and has set to music. They do not get on	In emotional turmoil, he still manages to complete the *Seventh Symphony* and compose the *Eighth Symphony*, as well as a *Violin Sonata* and *Three Equali for Four Trombones*	Napoleon makes the disastrous decision to march his *Grande Armée* to Moscow. It will lead to his biggest defeat and give the world the *1812 Overture*, by Tchaikovsky Wellington continues to inflict heavy defeats on the French in Spain, taking Madrid and forcing King Joseph (Napoleon's brother) to flee War of 1812 between US and UK Charles Dickens born

1813	Beethoven's brother falls ill with consumption, and declares that if he dies, Beethoven should become Karl's guardian He gives several public performances, including two charity concerts for the benefit of wounded soldiers	Persuaded by Mälzel (inventor of the metronome) to compose a piece for his Panharmonicon (mechanical orchestra) to celebrate Wellington's victory over the French at Vitoria	Wellington's decisive victory over the French at Vitoria in Spain, ensuring the end of the Peninsular War Napoleon himself decisively defeated by the allies at the Battle of Leipzig The Philharmonic Society of London established – it will later commission the *Ninth Symphony* from Beethoven Richard Wagner and Giuseppe Verdi born
1814	Beethoven agrees to revive his opera, to be performed – now as *Fidelio* – before foreign heads of state at the Congress of Vienna Takes part in a performance of his *Archduke Trio*, but his deafness ruins it. He will never perform in public again	The "big one" of the year is *Fidelio*. He also composes a *Cantata* for the Congress of Vienna, *The Glorious Moment*	April, Emperor Napoleon abdicates The Congress of Vienna is summoned to withdraw the map of post-Napoleonic Europe Napoleon is exiled to the island of Elba British troops burn Washington DC Adolphe Sax, inventor of the saxophone, is born
1815	Beethoven's brother Carl dies. Last-minute changes to his will force Beethoven to share guardianship of	He composes little, some *Overtures*, orchestral pieces, and two *Cello Sonatas*	Napoleon escapes from Elba, lands in France, and marches north, gathering an army

CONTINUED ▶

YEAR	What was happening to Beethoven?	What was Beethoven composing?	What else was going on in the world?
	Karl with the boy's mother. Beethoven begins a lawsuit that will last for over four years, break his health, and hamper his creativity enormously		The Battle of Waterloo, of course, and the end of Napoleon Louis XVIII restored to the French throne
1816	Beethoven wins the first round of the legal battle over Karl, and learns what it is like to be a single parent	He completes a *Piano Sonata* and his one great song cycle, *To the Immortal Beloved*, but there is little else	Rossini's *Barber of Seville* premiered in Rome
1817	Beethoven is ill for much of the year, and is having enormous problems with Karl, whom he has put into a boarding school in Vienna But some pleasure for him at the end of the year when he is visited by Thomas Broadwood, who promises to ship him a new Broadwood piano from London	The least creative year musically of Beethoven's life. But the promise of the Broadwood, together with Archduke Rudolph's approaching nameday, inspires him to begin a new *Piano Sonata*. It will become the mightiest of them all, the *Hammerklavier*	Social unrest across England Typhus epidemic in Ireland spreads to Edinburgh and Glasgow Tolstoy, Russian author, born Jane Austen dies
1818	Beethoven removes Karl from the boarding school to live with him. Disaster. The now severely deaf 47 year old cannot cope with a difficult 11 year old. Karl runs away to	With the new Broadwood piano in place, he completes the *Hammerklavier Sonata*, but that's about it for the year	John Ross makes his first Arctic voyage, searching for the North-West passage Mary Shelley writes *Frankenstein* *Silent Night* composed when church

	his mother. She uses this to reignite the court case. Beethoven makes the disastrous mistake of revealing in court he is not of noble birth. The Court of the Nobility hands the case down to the lower court. One bright note: the new Broadwood piano arrives, having been shipped to Trieste, then transported across the Alps		organs fail and first performed in Oberndorf, Austria. Karl Marx born
1819	The lower court finds against Beethoven, and he is forced to relinquish guardianship of Karl. His patron Archduke Rudolph is appointed Archbishop of Olmütz. Beethoven promises to compose a new piece for the enthronement, the *Missa Solemnis*	He begins work on the *Missa Solemnis*, but will miss Rudolph's enthronement by three years. Some canons and dances composed, but nothing of significance	Schubert composes his *Trout Quintet*. "Peterloo" massacre in Manchester – 11 killed and over 400 wounded. Franz von Suppé born. Jacques Offenbach born. Princess, later Queen, Victoria born
1820	Beethoven finally wins custody of Karl in the Court of Appeal. Johanna appeals unsuccessfully to the Emperor	Begins work on *Piano Sonata Op. 109*, and accepts a commission for three *Piano Sonatas*	First use of the conductor's baton at a concert in London. George III dies, succeeded by the Prince Regent as George IV. Jenny Lind, Swedish soprano, born

CONTINUED ▶

YEAR	What was happening to Beethoven?	What was Beethoven composing?	What else was going on in the world?
1821	Beethoven's health in serious decline. Rheumatic fever followed by jaundice. His lost love Josephine Brunsvik dies	The major work of the year is the *Piano Sonata Op. 110*. He also composes a set of *Piano Bagatelles*. Little else	Coronation of George IV. Napoleon dies in exile on the island of St Helena. Constable paints *The Hay Wain*
1822	Prince Galitzin commissions three *String Quartets* from Beethoven. They will become three of the great *Late Quartets*. The London Philharmonic Society offers Beethoven £50 for a new symphony. It will become the *Ninth*. Rossini visits Beethoven	The major work of the year is the *Piano Sonata Op. 111*. It will be his last. He also – finally – completes the *Missa Solemnis*, and does most of the work on the huge *Diabelli Variations*	Schubert's *"Unfinished" Symphony* composed. E.T.A. Hoffmann, music critic and champion of Beethoven's music, dies
1823	Beethoven applies to become Imperial and Royal Chamber Music Composer, but the post is abolished. He never held a paid job in all his years in Vienna. More ill health, including eye trouble	Extensive work on the *Ninth Symphony*, which will be his last. He completes the *Diabelli Variations*	The Monroe Doctrine excludes European powers from all interference in the political affairs of the US. Pushkin begins his greatest work, *Eugene Onegin*
1824	Beethoven presents his newly completed *Ninth Symphony* and parts of the *Missa Solemnis* at a concert on 7 May in the Kärntnertor theatre. He "conducts"	Completes the *Ninth Symphony*, and a final set of *Bagatelles* for piano. Composes the first of the three *String Quartets* for Galitzin, Op. 127	Schubert composes *Die schöne Müllerin*. Louis XVIII dies, to be succeeded by the reactionary Charles X. Smetana and Bruckner born

	alongside Unger. The contralto turns him round at the end of the *Ninth* to see the cheering and applause	Schubert composes his *"Great C major" Symphony* Johann Strauss junior, future Waltz King, born Death of Tsar Alexander, succeeded by his son, Tsar Nicholas Antonio Salieri dies
1825	Beethoven's health worsens dramatically and he learns that Karl has been secretly seeing his mother Sir George Smart conducts the first English performance of the *Ninth Symphony*. Beethoven had intended coming to London to conduct himself, but ill health prevented him In October Beethoven moves to the *Schwarzspanierhaus*, his final lodging	Completes two more *String Quartets*, *Opp. 132 & 130* (in that order). Together with *Opus 131* they surpass anything he has written for string quartet before. Longer, more intense, and regarded as the pinnacle of string quartet composition Makes sketches for a *Tenth Symphony*, which will remain unwritten
1826	Beethoven again suffering from abdominal and eye complaints First performance of the *String Quartet Op. 130*. Not a success. Beethoven agrees to hive off the final movement, the mighty *Grosse Fuge*, and publish it separately Karl, having had enough of his uncle's attempts to control every aspect of his life, pawns his watch, buys two pistols	He composes the *String Quartets Opp. 131 & 135*. He also composes a final movement for Op. 130 to replace the *Grosse Fuge*. It is the last complete piece of music he will compose	Weber dies in London Mendelssohn writes his overture, *A Midsummer Night's Dream* University of London founded

CONTINUED ▶

23

YEAR	What was happening to Beethoven?	What was Beethoven composing?	What else was going on in the world?
	and gunpowder, goes to Baden and attempts to commit suicide, succeeding only in wounding himself in the head Later in the year Beethoven takes Karl to stay with brother Johann on his country estate in Gneixendorf. After two months, they travel back to Vienna in an open-top cart. By the time they arrive in Vienna, Beethoven is critically ill		
1827	Karl leaves to take up military service In late March Beethoven is given the last rites 26 March, at approximately 5.45 pm, during a thunderstorm in Vienna, Beethoven dies 29 March 20,000 people line the streets as the funeral cortege passes by He is buried at Währing cemetery, northwest of the city. Sixty-one years later his body will be exhumed and reburied in the Musicians' Quarter of Vienna Central Cemetery, where he lies today		

02

The Story of Beethoven: The Cast List

Major roles

Beethoven: *the male lead*

The eldest son, born into a musical family, his talent recognized early by his father. Spent his childhood and teenage years in his home town of Bonn, leaving for his second visit to Vienna just before his 22nd birthday. He never returned. Rapidly established himself as the finest piano virtuoso the city had seen, and soon came to be recognized as its foremost composer. Dominated Vienna's musical scene until his death at the age of 56. 20,000 people lined the streets for his funeral.

Ludwig: *the grandfather*

Kapellmeister at the court in Bonn. Beethoven was only 3 when he died, but he remained devoted to him for the rest of his life.

Johann: *the father*

Tenor at the court in Bonn, but failed to succeed his father as *Kapellmeister*. Became an alcoholic and was dismissed from court service. As he became more and more incapable, Beethoven had to take over the running of the family.

Maria Magdalena: *the mother*

Soon realized she was trapped in an unhappy marriage. She died of consumption at the age of 40. Her ill health prevented Beethoven remaining in Vienna, where he had come aged 16, to study with Mozart.

Johanna: *the sister-in-law*

Wife of Beethoven's brother Carl and mother of his nephew Karl. Beethoven believed her to be a wicked and immoral woman, based on her conviction for stealing. After Carl's death, Beethoven fought for

more than four years in the courts to exclude her from the guardianship of Karl. She was not nearly as bad as he had come to believe.

Karl: *the nephew*

Following brother Carl's wishes, Beethoven assumed guardianship of the boy on his father's death. Successfully fought Johanna in the courts to retain the guardianship, but made an absolute hash of bringing the boy up. He smothered the boy with an overwhelming love, forcing Karl ultimately to exact terrible revenge.

Stephan von Breuning: *the friend*

Beethoven's closest, longest, and most loyal friend. Knew him from childhood in Bonn, and the friendship continued in Vienna. At one point Beethoven and Stephan shared an apartment in Vienna. Despite frequent ruptures in the relationship, all Beethoven's fault, Stephan remained loyal. He died only months after Beethoven, and his son blamed his early death on the strain of caring for his famous and difficult friend.

Minor roles

Caspar Carl: *the brother*

Elder of Beethoven's two younger brothers. Followed Beethoven to Vienna in 1794, tried to earn a living teaching music, but eventually took a job as clerk in the finance department. He died at the age of just 41 of consumption. Father of Karl, the only Beethoven of the next generation.

Nikolaus Johann: *the brother*

Younger of Beethoven's two brothers. Became a wealthy pharmacist. Beethoven did all he could to stop Johann marrying his housekeeper. Bought country estate where Beethoven and Karl stayed in the autumn of 1826. Survived his brother by 21 years.

Antonie Brentano: *the lover(?)*

Strongest candidate for the Immortal Beloved, the only woman, as far as we know, who ever physically returned Beethoven's love. She was in both the right places – Prague and Karlsbad – at the right time – first week of July 1812.

Haydn: *the composer*

Beethoven's first teacher in Vienna. The relationship had its problems. Beethoven, dissatisfied, secretly took lessons with someone else. Haydn, in his 60s, was incredibly busy and had difficulty finding time for his precocious young pupil. But Beethoven always held Haydn in high regard.

Neefe: *the teacher*

Beethoven's first full-time teacher. He quickly recognized the boy's extraordinary talent, securing for him the post of assistant organist. He taught him to play Bach and encouraged his early attempts at composition.

Ries: *the helper*

Worked tirelessly as Beethoven's assistant in Vienna. Came to live in London and was instrumental in securing the commission from the London Philharmonic Society for what was to be the *Ninth Symphony.*

Archduke Rudolph: *the patron*

Beethoven's greatest patron. Younger brother of the emperor. An accomplished musician, he was the only pupil Beethoven ever took on as a composition student. Paid Beethoven an annuity to persuade him to remain in Vienna. Beethoven dedicated more compositions to Archduke Rudolph than to any other single person.

Count Waldstein: *the patron*

Beethoven's first patron in Bonn. Instrumental in securing Beethoven's second and conclusive trip to Vienna, writing in Beethoven's autograph book that he would receive "Mozart's spirit from Haydn's hands". Beethoven immortalized his name with the *Waldstein Sonata*.

Various extras

George Bridgetower

Virtuoso violinist. He came to Vienna in 1803 and Beethoven composed the famous *Violin Sonata Op. 47* for him. The two gave it its first performance. But they later fell out and Beethoven sent the sonata to the French violinist whose name it now bears: Rudolphe Kreutzer.

Josephine Brunsvik

Beethoven took her on as a pupil and fell in love with her, writing a series of letters to her asking for a physical relationship. She rejected him, but later came to regret it.

Giulietta Guicciardi

Another of Beethoven's loves, once again a pupil. It seems she reciprocated. Beethoven proposed, she apparently accepted, but her father forbade the marriage. Beethoven dedicated to her the piano sonata now known as *The Moonlight*.

Prince Lichnowsky

Beethoven's first important patron in Vienna. Beethoven lived with the prince and his wife when he first came to Vienna. Beethoven dedicated several compositions to him.

Prince Lobkowitz

Another important patron in Vienna. Beethoven gave the first public performance of the *Eroica Symphony* in Lobkowitz's concert room, and dedicated the work to him after scratching out the original dedicatee's name – Napoleon Bonaparte – on the title page.

Therese Malfatti

Another pupil with whom Beethoven fell in love. Almost certainly composed the famous *Bagatelle* known today as *Für Elise* for her.

Mozart

Too important to be a "various extra", I know, but Beethoven and Mozart met just once. Beethoven was 16, and had come to Vienna to meet and study with Mozart. After hearing the boy play, Mozart agreed to take him on, but Beethoven had to return to Bonn where his mother was terminally ill.

Napoleon Bonaparte

Probably the first time Napoleon (like Mozart) has ever been a "various extra" in anything. Beethoven admired him and originally dedicated the *Eroica Symphony* to him, but exploded with rage when Napoleon declared himself Emperor – *he is a tyrant after all* – and scratched his name from the title page.

Prince Razumovsky

Russian ambassador to the Habsburg court in Vienna, and accomplished amateur violinist. Commissioned the three string quartets now known as the *Razumovsky Quartets*.

Anton Schindler

Lawyer and violinist who was very close to Beethoven for a period late in the composer's life. Wrote unreliable memoirs about Beethoven, destroyed many of the conversation books and sanitized others to preserve his master's reputation. Beethoven disliked him, but came to rely on his dedication and efficiency.

Dr Wawruch

Looked after Beethoven in his final illness and left a vivid account of Beethoven's final months.

Franz Wegeler

Childhood friend in Bonn, who later became
a qualified doctor. In a letter to Wegeler, Beethoven
first admitted that he was going deaf.

The Spaniard

A Difficult Arrival

Ludwig van Beethoven was born on . . . That's the
first problem we face in chronicling this remarkable
life. We do not know for certain the day on which
Beethoven was born. That is just the first difficulty of
many we shall have to grapple with in a life that lasted
for 56 years, three months, and around two weeks.

What we *do* know is that on 17 December 1770 the
infant son of Johann and Maria Magdalena van
Beethoven was christened at the church of
St Remigius in Bonn, and named Ludwig after his
paternal grandfather. It was the custom for babies

to be baptized within 24 hours of birth, and so we can say with near certainty that Beethoven was born on 16 December. "Near" certainty, because it was not unknown for baptism to take place 48 hours later, particularly if the birth was difficult, or on the same day if the birth happened in the early hours of the morning. So 15 and 17 December remain possibilities.

Does it matter? Yes, to many Beethoven devotees it does. So often I am told by proud audience members at my Beethoven talks that they share a birthday with Beethoven, and the date they always give is 17 December. They are probably one day out – for most that is close enough.

The reason we cannot be sure is that Beethoven's birth certificate does not exist, or at least no longer exists, very probably for the simple reason that his father was an idle and heavy-drinking man who lost it. He would not be alone – many family records from that era are incomplete. There is another possibility, altogether more sinister, and it is worth leaping ahead in time to examine it.

When Johann put his son forward to give his first public recital, he announced the boy's age on a printed poster as 6 when he was in fact 7¼. Could a father make such a mistake about the age of his eldest son? Or was it a deliberate ruse to exaggerate the skill and precocity of the child, and thus turn him into the family breadwinner – as another young child had become for *his* family not many years before, a certain Wolfgang Amadeus Mozart? If that was the case, Johann certainly would have destroyed the evidence, namely the birth certificate.

What we do know is that, until middle age, Beethoven believed himself to be two years younger than he was. *Two?* Well, first there is the father's fiction, that he must have maintained, (thereby strengthening the suspicion that it was deliberate), and, second, as anyone born in December knows, you are always one year younger than the date of your birth suggests. *(It's true. If your birthday is in December 1980, in 2005 you are 24, not 25, for 11 months of the year.)*

Back to the arrival into the world of our subject, and I said he was the eldest son of the Beethovens, but he was not the first-born. That was also a boy, also Ludwig, born in the previous year, and who lived for just a week. Five more children followed after *our* Ludwig, of whom only two, both boys, lived into adulthood.

The Beethovens thus had three sons, of whom the future composer was the eldest. Ludwig was a quiet, withdrawn child, who found it difficult to make friends, not least with his own brothers. Throughout his life he argued and frequently fell out with them, regarding them both (not unreasonably) as idiots and imbeciles. There is very little anecdotal evidence of his relationship with his parents. Nothing, in fact, to suggest he grew up in a warm, loving home atmosphere.

The fault was more likely his than theirs. What genius is easy to live with? From as soon as he understood speech, the sounds in his head were musical notes, not words. Talking to him, reasoning with him, must have been a nightmare. Thus was a lifelong pattern set early.

Ludwig the First

No, not the baby who died at a week old, but the most important Ludwig in *our* Ludwig's life, his grandfather.

Ludwig van Beethoven (senior) was born in Mechelen in Flanders (now Malines in Belgium), which accounts for the *van* not *von* in the family name. A good treble voice broke into a fine bass, and in 1733, at the age of 21, he was invited by the Elector of Cologne to move to Bonn to take up the position of court musician.

The Beethoven family can be traced in Flanders back to the early Middle Ages. The name means "beet yard", suggesting early members of the family were vegetable farmers. The name exists in the records in various forms, Bethowe, Bethoven, Bettehove, Bierthoven, Beerthoven, becoming established for the first time as Beethoven in the early 1500s.

He settled in Bonn where, 28 years later, he was promoted to the exalted position of *Kapellmeister*, head of all court music. By the time his grandson was born nearly a decade later, the *Kapellmeister* was one of the most distinguished and highly respected burghers of Bonn.

The infant Ludwig attached himself to his grandfather, who would walk proudly with his small grandson along the neatly tended paths of the palace grounds, nodding to acquaintances and colleagues, and introducing the small boy as – shall we speculate? – a future musician.

No wonder the child cleaved to his grandfather. His father was useless.

Johann the Sprinter

Well, maybe not entirely useless, but no earth shaker either. Johann van Beethoven had inherited his father's musical talent, in the form of a good voice, and was able to secure employment as a tenor in the court choir. This gave him a regular salary, which he supplemented by giving singing lessons.

But it is clear that home life was not good. Johann spent a lot of time out drinking with his friends (chief among them Klein the fishmonger), and would sometimes stay out all night, even taking

himself off for days at a time, returning penitent
and the worse for wear.

Maria Magdalena, by contrast, was quiet and
thoughtful – and deeply disappointed in the man
she had married. She once said to the daughter of
a neighbour:

*If you want to take my good advice, remain single, and
then you will have the most tranquil, most beautiful,
most pleasurable life. For what is marriage? A little joy,
but then a chain of sorrows.*

There were plenty of links in Maria Magdalena's
own "chain of sorrows". She lost her father when
she was just 12, and then married for the first time
only a month past her 16th birthday. She quickly
gave birth to a son, who died in infancy, and within
less than two years of marriage her husband was
dead too.

She then found herself being wooed by a musician,
an artist, and fell under his spell. Both Maria
Magdalena's mother and Johann's father were dead
set against the marriage, but the young couple
ignored their pleadings and married.

Once again she swiftly became pregnant, giving
birth to the Ludwig who only survived for a week.
So when our Ludwig was born, his mother had
already lost two children and a husband, and was

beginning to realize too that her second marriage was a mistake.

Johann clearly loved his wife – or certainly *had* – since he met her in a town some distance upriver from Bonn, and made the time-consuming journey again and again to carry out his courtship.

What, then, came between Johann and his young wife? Why, the demon drink. Johann's father, the *Kapellmeister*, made a little bit of money on the side dabbling in the wine trade, thus there were always boxes of wine in the house. Johann was not the first victim of this ready supply. His mother had become an alcoholic, and had to move out of the family home to receive treatment. He himself not only grew used to having wine at home, but was also frequently given wine as a gift by grateful students who no doubt knew the pleasure he derived from it.

The pleasure came at a severe cost, though. When the new Elector ordered a review of all court musical activities, the report stated that:

Johann van Beethoven has a very stale voice, has been long in the service, is very poor, of fair deportment, and married.

That stale voice did for him. His father had cruelly nicknamed him *Johann der Läufer*, *Johann the Sprinter*, telling him once:

41

Keep running, keep running. You will some day run to your final destination.

Johann knew in his mind what that destination was, and when his father died he waited for the good news that he had been chosen to succeed him as *Kapellmeister*.

The letter never came. Johann's career was over. His father's death, therefore, marked a turning point for Johann, after which it was all downhill.

For his eldest son, his grandfather's death was a tragedy which marked him for life. Ludwig, *our* Ludwig, was just a week or so past his third birthday when the old man died, and so some of his earliest memories were of his grandfather.

The *Kapellmeister* saw early on that Johann would never make the grade as a musician, and so he pinned his hopes on his eldest grandson, who bore his name.

We can safely assume that it was from his grandfather that young Ludwig first heard the names of Bach, Handel, and the young genius making such an impression in Vienna, Mozart. From his grandfather that he first heard talk of music. And indeed that it was his grandfather's singing voice that produced the first musical sounds he heard.

On the wall of the Beethoven apartment in Bonn
hung a portrait of Ludwig van Beethoven,
Kapellmeister. As our Ludwig grew up, in a
household in which his father was succumbing to
alcoholism, in which his mother moved sadly and
consumed with melancholy, one can imagine the
boy – silent, engrossed in his own world – standing
in front of the portrait, trying to come to terms
with his loss.

Johann pawned that portrait. Not very many years
later, making his mark as a musician in Vienna,
Ludwig sent money back to a friend in Bonn, with
orders to retrieve the portrait and forward it to him
in Vienna.

The portrait of Ludwig's grandfather then hung on
the wall of every apartment he lived in for the rest
of his life, and was on the wall of the room in
which he died.

A Good Teacher

Johann van Beethoven was not entirely beyond
rational thought. As a trained musician it did not
take him long to realize that his eldest son was
rather talented. While he was earning reasonable
money, he had moved the family out of the tiny
two-bedroom apartment in which Ludwig was born,
into a spacious apartment on the second floor of a
large house just a few paces away from the banks of

the Rhine. The house was owned by Fischer, the master baker, and in it there was . . . a piano.

Watching his small son tinkering with the keys, quickly producing tunes, he swiftly realized that Ludwig might just be good enough to become a potential source of income. If Leopold Mozart could make money out of his son, why should he not try the same trick?

So he made a decision. A good decision. He hired a teacher for Ludwig. Pity it was a bad teacher. Tobias Pfeiffer was an oboist and flautist, who could play a good tune and drink a good drink.

Johann was pleased to have a new drinking companion, and the two men would spend most evenings in the tavern, returning to the house late at night and drunk.

According to one of the Fischer children (whose memoirs of Beethoven's childhood are the most

Fischer recounts a wonderful anecdote from these early years. There was a well-known eccentric in Bonn by the name of Stumpf (Fischer calls him Stommb), a former musician who had become senile. This man had taken to walking through the streets of the town, in his right hand a baton, in his left a roll of music. Without speaking, he would approach the Fischer house in the Rheingasse, walk into the entrance hall,

comprehensive account we have of this crucial
formative period, even if they were written more
than half a century later), Johann and Pfeiffer, after
a long evening's drinking, would get back to the
house, where they would find young Ludwig asleep:

*His father would shake him awake and the crying
child would go to the piano, where Pfeiffer would sit
with him until morning, because he could see that he
was talented.*

This brief account has led to the traditionally
accepted image of a tyrannical father dragging a
crying boy to the piano, rapping him across the
knuckles, forcing him to play for hour after hour in
the night.

It was almost certainly not that bad. Pfeiffer
himself was a capable musician, and Gottfried
Fischer makes a point of saying that when Pfeiffer
and Ludwig played together – Pfeiffer on flute,
Ludwig accompanying him on piano – the sounds

*and bang on the table with his baton, all the time not saying
a word. He would then point up to the Beethoven apartment
and beat with his baton on the music roll, as if to indicate
that a fellow musician lived up there. Ludwig knew about
this and used to laugh. On one occasion he said: "Now we
can see what happens to musicians. Music has already driven
this one mad, and it'll probably do the same to us."*

they made were so beautiful people would stop in the street outside to listen. It is therefore probable Ludwig quite liked Pfeiffer and enjoyed his teaching. No child wants to be woken up by a drunken father, but Johann then probably staggered off to bed, leaving Ludwig to do what he loved best, and Pfeiffer to sit there and marvel.

Just as well, though, that Pfeiffer had to leave Bonn after a year, leaving Ludwig without a teacher.

Enter Christian Gottlob Neefe, a composer and keyboard player who had come to Bonn with his young family and secured employment as court organist, as well as music director with the local theatrical company.

No one knows what persuaded Johann to employ Neefe to teach Ludwig, but it was an inspired choice. Neefe immediately recognized an unusual talent in the boy, and set about nurturing it. The biggest stroke of good fortune for Ludwig was that Neefe was a composer, and when he began to scribble down his own first efforts at composition, Neefe encouraged him. Too much, in fact. One of his few friends later said:

Our Ludwig frequently complained of the too severe criticisms made of his first efforts in composition.

You'll note I said one of his "few" friends. I've already described a lonely childhood. It was made a lot more lonely by Johann's appallingly selfish decision to take Ludwig out of school when he was just 10 years old so he could concentrate on music. Beethoven bore the scars for life. His handwriting was dreadful – so bad in later years that there has sometimes been doubt about the authenticity of letters and manuscripts. His spelling, use of punctuation and capital letters (these last two very important in the highly structured German language) were all over the place. He would often ask someone more educated to write important letters for him.

Not that Ludwig will have minded too much being taken out of school. He hated it there. What solitary boy with his head full ever makes friends at school? Years later several of those at school with him wrote their reminiscences. They talk of a "shy and taciturn" boy. Not one relates games played with him, not one describes him as a playfellow, not one talks of walking in the hills or adventures in boats on the Rhine with him.

On one occasion Ludwig turned up for school in a dreadful state. His clothes were unkempt and clearly in need of repair. One of the boys teased him, saying the only explanation for his state was that his mother must be dead. Can you imagine how hurtful such a remark would be to an 8- or 9-year-old boy?

And then there was the nickname. Among blond haired, pale-skinned, no doubt tallish Aryan boys, Ludwig, with his darker skin and tousled dark hair, his shorter stockier frame, stood apart. So they called him "The Spaniard". What schoolboy likes being singled out as different? Already aware that he was somehow not like them, unable to join in with the rest of them in schoolboy pranks, he was driven even further into isolation by their cruel teasing.

Was Beethoven black? It is a question that has long been debated, and in the late 20th century several civil rights groups claimed him as their own. The most we can say on the issue is that the Beethoven family lived in Flanders, which was overrun by the Spanish in the late 1500s and became part of the Spanish Netherlands. The Spanish army contained soldiers who were Moors, dark-skinned North Africans whose families had stayed when the Moors invaded Spain centuries before. As part of the occupying army in the Netherlands, Moorish, as well as Spanish, soldiers settled, married and had children. It is

And so when Johann took his son out of school and handed him over to Neefe, he is unlikely to have encountered any fierce opposition.

Neefe was acutely aware of all this, and saw his role as more than just musical training. And this is where the first element of danger comes into Ludwig's life. Neefe was a Protestant, from the town of Chemnitz in Saxony. He was therefore not only an outsider, but of the wrong religion too. It does not take too much imagination to see Neefe talking for long hours to his young pupil about music, philosophy, religion, politics, to broaden his intellectual horizons beyond the small traditional confines of Bonn . . . or to see Ludwig listening with attention and admiration to his teacher.

Neefe also believed strongly that music was not an art form divorced from life, the creation simply of

therefore possible that the Beethoven family absorbed Moorish, or Spanish, blood. Certainly early portraits of Beethoven show facial characteristics compatible with this. There is also plenty of anecdotal evidence. There was the school nickname, for a start, and several contemporaries wrote of what they called Beethoven's "negroid" features. Some musicologists too point to the unusual rhythms and harmonies with which Beethoven took music in a new direction, and suggest this might be to do with a more cosmopolitan background than a straightforwardly Flemish ancestry would have given him.

nice tunes and sounds. He believed music was part of the spiritual life of man. Given that Beethoven was to become the first composer to embody this idea, we can see just what an important influence Neefe was.

It was under Neefe's instruction that Ludwig began his first attempts at composition. It was also from Neefe that he first heard radical ideas. In all senses Neefe was the most formative individual in Ludwig's early life.

Within a year of beginning lessons with Neefe, Ludwig published his first composition, a set of variations on a march by another composer. A year later he published the first work that was truly his own. It was a set of three piano sonatas that he dedicated to the Elector, and thus known today as the *Kurfürsten Sonatas WoO 47* (WoO standing for *Werke ohne Opuszahl, Work without Opus number*). Even if we take into account that Neefe will have guided him, the sonatas are an utterly remarkable piece of work for a 12-year-old boy.

In the following year, Neefe once again proved his worth. He secured for Ludwig the position of assistant court organist on a salary of 150 florins. It was Ludwig's first paid employment. When Neefe was called on to stand in as *Kapellmeister*, which meant full-time administrative duties, Ludwig took over not only as organist at all the religious services at court, but stood in as pianist at rehearsals of the stage company, which involved directing from the keyboard.

Neefe was turning his young pupil into a musician. Neefe was one of those men whom history forgets, but whose place in history is secured by what they did for others. He was not a genius, but had the good sense not only to be aware of that fact, but to recognize it – without envy – in someone else, even the unlikely figure of a child.

On 2 March 1783 he wrote a letter to a music journal that for the first time links his pupil to that certain other composer, already recognized as an unqualified musical genius, and dares to use the same word about him:

This youthful genius is deserving of help to enable him to travel. He would surely become a second Wolfgang Amadeus Mozart were he to continue as he has begun.

In later years Beethoven himself expressed his appreciation to Neefe, in a letter that demonstrates how much more natural he was at writing notes than words:

I thank you for your advice, which you very often gave me as I advanced in my heavenly art.

A Good Patron

A good teacher is a help, but in this age of aristocrats and patronage a good patron is essential. Please welcome onto the stage Count Ferdinand Ernst Gabriel Waldstein und Wartemberg von Dux, known to history as Count Waldstein.

The count had the good fortune to be born into one of the most noble, aristocratic and wealthy families in the Habsburg empire, and the bad fortune to be the younger son. As such he was packed off to one of the outposts of empire, a small

sleepy town somewhere off to the west by the name
of Bonn in the German principality of Cologne and
Münster.

This was not altogether bad news for him. He was a
personal friend of the new Elector (both were
Knights of the austere sounding Teutonic Order, an
organization dating back to the Crusades which had
become little more than a drinking club for
testosterone-fuelled young Teutons), and shared
with him a profound love of the arts, in particular
music.

The new Elector set about reorganizing musical
activity at court, and it was his order for a report on
every musician employed at court that sank Johann
van Beethoven's chances of succeeding his father as
Kapellmeister.

Count Waldstein arrived in Bonn in late January
1788, keen to find something or someone –
preferably musical – to spend his generous family
allowance on, and found it in the form of a 17-year-
old boy whose musical reputation was growing by
the day.

The timing was not just fortuitous, it was
something of a lifesaver. For the boy Waldstein
found was not, as you might expect, a happy
confident teenager indulging his passion for music,
playing, composing, and forging a career.

Ludwig van Beethoven had just experienced an *annus horribilis*. 1787 had begun with such hope. In the spring he had embarked on a trip to Vienna which was nothing short of a childhood dream come true. (I shall keep you in suspense for a few pages more about what it was – clue: *Mozart.*) His father, having failed to get the top job, was rapidly descending into alcoholism (enforced retirement was not far off). On 17 July he suffered the greatest trauma a teenage boy can surely know: his mother died. Four months later, in a shambolic household that must have reeked of alcohol, his 1-year-old sister died, probably through neglect.

As this terrible year yielded to a new one, Ludwig was living in poverty, was trying to come to terms with the loss of his mother and the failure of his father, was melancholle, despondent, ashamed, depressed, and frequently ill.

Thank goodness for Count Waldstein, who took the boy out of himself, talked music to him, ate and drank with him, introduced him to the salons of the very highest rank of the nobility – and without any doubt pushed money onto the impoverished family. A childhood friend calls him *"Beethoven's Maecenas"*.

Ludwig was to repay him in an extraordinary way – actually not that extraordinary for the time, but truly extraordinary given what we know of Beethoven's character.

Count Waldstein took it upon himself to organize an extravagant entertainment to celebrate Carnival Sunday on 6 March 1791. The nobility of Bonn would process through the Marktplatz in traditional German costume, and stage a ballet in the Ridotto Room of the electoral palace – "ballet" meaning the taking up of theatrical poses with little or no movement. The scenes would represent traditional elements of German life – war, the hunt, love, drinking . . .

. . . To musical accompaniment, of course. Waldstein turned to his young protégé and asked him if would compose the music. He asked him something else too. Would Ludwig mind awfully if he let it be known that he, Waldstein, was actually the composer?

A huge cheek, we might think today, but this sort of thing was not actually that unusual at the time.

Count Waldstein lived a chequered life. He got himself into huge debt trying to raise a regiment to fight the French, and was reportedly in Paris incognito (to evade his creditors) in 1802. It is possible he came to Vienna soon after, though there is no record of a meeting with Beethoven. But Waldstein's money problems were common knowledge among his friends, and it is possible Beethoven thought dedicating a piano sonata to him would help.

He married a wealthy Polish countess, managing to spend much of her money to no good purpose. He took out a loan

Remember, the commission for Mozart's *Requiem* came from a count who wished to publish the work under his own name, and Mozart agreed.

So did the young, needy Ludwig van Beethoven. He composed a splendid set of *scena*, under titles such as Hunting Song, Love Song, War Dance, Drinking Song. For much of the 19th century it was believed Count Waldstein really was the composer. It was not until late in the century that scholars rectified matters, and the *Musik zu einem Ritterballet (Music for a Ballet of Knights)* was attributed to the 19-year-old Ludwig, and accorded the significant number *WoO 1*.

He repaid him in another way too – the best way a composer can repay anyone. He dedicated his great *Piano Sonata Op. 53* to Waldstein, so that Waldstein's

against her fortune, and was unable to repay it. She died in 1818, deeply depressed and resigned to her husband's failure. He then took over his mother-in-law's business, managing to bankrupt that too.

He died in some squalor in 1823, in a strange bed and a strange house, unable to afford a doctor. On the day of his death news reached him that his elder brother had died, making him heir to the family fortune.

A Good Friend

So, Ludwig had a good teacher and a good patron. What young man can do without a good friend too? And if you have very few anyway, it is all the more important. Ludwig was lucky. He had the best friend possible, a few years younger than him, who was loyal, honest, and caring to Ludwig throughout both their lives. Ludwig repaid him with disloyalty, false accusations, and bitterness – all totally undeserved.

At the top of the largest square in Bonn, the Münsterplatz, there stands the most imposing statue of Beethoven anywhere in the world. Stand in front of it today, look off to your left, ignore the garish supermarket, and try to imagine a beautiful wide two-storey house, no fewer than nine

The massive bronze statue shows Beethoven at the height of his maturity, full length, larger than life size, one leg ahead of the other, both feet planted firmly on the ground, a pen in his lowered right hand and a notebook in his left, brow knitted, features concentrating, abundantly thick hair framing his head.

For its ceremonial unveiling in 1845 the guests of honour were no lesser figures than Queen Victoria and Prince Albert,

name will live on for as long as Beethoven's music is played. In other words, for ever.

windows across the first floor, ornate gable windows set into an imposing roof, an ornate fence around a small front garden closing it off from passers-by.

This house was home to the von Breuning family, one of the most cultured in Bonn – a house the young Ludwig probably spent more time in than his own, as family problems grew worse.

We don't know exactly when or how Ludwig met his great friend Stephan von Breuning – probably shortly before or soon after his mother died when he was 16 – but it was a friendship that would last (with frequent ruptures, all of them down to Beethoven) for the rest of his life.

The friendship began when Helene von Breuning, recently widowed matriarch of the family, employed Ludwig to teach piano to her children. This brought Ludwig a little extra cash, which he

---

the King and Queen of Prussia, and an Austrian archduke. They were seated on the balcony that had been specially erected on the front of the house of Count von Fürstenburg, now the post office headquarters. When, to cheers from the crowd, the beating of drums, the ringing of bells, and the firing of cannon, the statue was unveiled, it was found – to the embarrassment of the city dignitaries of Bonn – to be facing down the square, its back to the guests of honour on the balcony.

could well do with, but more importantly gave him every excuse he needed to absent himself from his alcoholic father and the two brothers with whom he had absolutely nothing in common.

Frau von Breuning instructed the servants that the dishevelled, unkempt boy was to be allowed into the house whenever he wished, and was to be permitted to go into the music room and play on the piano at all times. In short, they were to treat him like her own children.

He repaid her by being difficult and unpredictable. If he failed to turn up for a lesson, or cancelled one at the last minute, she would simply smile and say:

He has his raptus *again.*

As his skills as a musician became more widely known in Bonn, and more and more people began to demand his time, she regarded it as her role to protect him. Ludwig remembered her kindness. Late in life, speaking of her, he said with lack of modesty:

She understood how to keep the insects off the flowers.

There is no doubt that the eldest daughter of the von Breuning family, Eleonore, was Ludwig's

first love. It is easy to imagine him, an awkward
teenage boy becoming aware of girls, sitting
alongside her at the piano, no doubt the closest
he had ever been to a girl, charmed by her voice,
breathing her scent, becoming consumed by
teenage passion.

*Soon after he left Bonn for good, he wrote to Eleonore
apologizing for his appalling behaviour. She responded with
forgiveness, sending him a knitted waistcoat. What had
happened? We do not know. I am in no doubt that when he
went to bid her farewell, he tried to kiss her, probably in a
lunging, ungainly way, and was rebuffed.*

*Eleonore went on to marry Ludwig's other great childhood
friend, Franz Wegeler, and although Beethoven corresponded
with them late in life, after he left Bonn he never saw either
of them again.*

Stephan moved to Vienna soon after Ludwig, and,
with breaks, lived there for the rest of his life. He
was always ready to help his friend, get him out of
trouble, smooth frayed nerves, repair damaged
relationships. On one occasion Ludwig moved into
Stephan's apartment to live with him, forgot to
cancel the lease on his own apartment in the same
building, and when the landlord demanded
payment he accused Stephan of cheating him out of
money. It led to the most serious rift between them,
but as always Stephan ensured it was not
permanent.

Stephan's first wife died tragically young, after less than a year of marriage. The son of his second marriage, who became a doctor, has left us the most vivid account we have of Beethoven's declining years. He states that his father died within less than three months of his great and famous friend, and attributes the sudden collapse in his health to the strain of caring for him for so long.

The Greatest Composer

Now back to that trip of a lifetime which saw the *annus horribilis* of 1787 begin with such promise. Incredibly, unbelievably, the Elector – in whose orchestra, as well as all his other duties, Ludwig played viola! – gave him limited leave of absence to go Vienna to meet and study with . . . Mozart.

Imagine the boy, barely turned 16, packing his bag and leaving his home town, his family, for the first time, to make the long coach journey east to the capital city of music, Vienna, knowing that he was going to meet the greatest living composer.

It is perhaps surprising, certainly tantalizing, that we know so little of what happened when they met. It is even more surprising that in later years Beethoven barely referred to the meeting, as if, perhaps, he did not want to be seen in the shadow of the great man.

Let us piece together what we do know, and recreate the scene when the two greatest names in all classical music met.

Mozart   *All right, sit at the piano and play something. Be quick. I am busy.*
[Beethoven walks to the piano, praying his knees will not collapse, a tightness in his chest, butterflies in his stomach, his fingers trembling with nerves. He sits, digs his nails into his thighs to calm his fingers, then stretches them forward and plays. For several minutes his fingers fly across the keys with dazzling virtuosity.]

Mozart   *Hmm, impressive, but you obviously prepared it earlier, practised it, worked at it. It shows nothing, gives me no idea if —*

Beethoven   *Herr Mozart, please. Give me a tune. Come here and give me a tune. Any tune. And I will improvise on it.*
[Mozart goes to the piano and plays a tune of his own invention, something Beethoven cannot possibly have heard before. Beethoven smiles, in his element now, and improvises on it. On and on he plays, unpicking it and putting it back together again, slow, fast, loud, soft, always the original theme discernible underneath. Finally he brings it to a close. Mozart, without speaking, gets up and opens the door into the adjoining room where his wife Constanze is entertaining guests. Pointing back, he says to them:]

Mozart   *Watch out for that boy. One day he will
give the world something to talk about.*
[He goes up to Beethoven.]

*Boy, your playing was dreadful. You hack
at the keys as if you are chopping wood.
You pound on the piano as if it is your
worst enemy. But I confess I did not hear
a wrong note. Come back here in two
days. I will teach you.*

Ludwig returned to his lodgings, I imagine, with a
cushion of air between the soles of his feet and the
cobbles . . . to find an urgent letter from his father
telling him to return to Bonn immediately, without
wasting a single hour. His mother was ill with
consumption, desperately ill, and they feared for
her life.

What choice did Ludwig have? He had to return.
And so he never took lessons with the composer
he admired above all others. What if he had? Might
Mozart, the perfectionist, have smoothed off the
rough edges, tamed the wild spirit? Possibly.
Who knows? There is no doubt that for the 16-year-
old boy it was a disaster. For us, maybe not so.

It was to be another five and a half years before
Ludwig returned to Vienna, by which time Mozart
was dead.

By now adult, famous throughout Bonn as a
virtuoso, with a growing reputation as composer,

crucial member of the court orchestra, salaried
court organist, it was far more difficult to persuade
the Elector to let him travel.

This time it was undoubtedly Count Waldstein who
made it possible, taking advantage of the chaos
caused by renewed war against France, which made it
necessary for the Elector and nobility to vacate Bonn
for their own safety, and the court orchestra to be
disbanded. With the situation deteriorating so
rapidly, he reasoned, surely the absence of a mere 21-
year-old musician would not be felt? Added to this,
another renowned composer who had recently passed
through Bonn had offered to take Ludwig on as a
pupil if he could be sent to Vienna, namely Franz
Joseph Haydn. So why not let him go? The Elector,
with more pressing matters on his mind, agreed.
Thus Waldstein secured Ludwig's gratitude once and
for all and, with the dedication of that *Piano Sonata*,
ensured the immortality of his name.

On 2 November 1792, just one month short of his
22nd birthday, Ludwig van Beethoven bade his
father and brothers a no doubt brusque farewell,
assuring them he would return within a year, and
boarded a coach for the first leg of the trip to
Vienna – a dangerous journey which would take
him close to both a friendly army and the enemy.

The coach travelled south along the banks of
the Rhine, and at the small town of

Ehrenbreitstein – his mother's home town – it swung east, giving Ludwig his last look at the mighty river on whose banks he and his brothers had grown up.

He probably didn't take much notice, knowing he would soon be back. He never saw the Rhine again, or Bonn. Or his father, who died the following month.

In the days before he left, Ludwig went round to the people he knew and asked them to sign his autograph book. (Probably the moment he made the ill-advised lunge at Eleonore.) Waldstein thus became the second person after Neefe to acknowledge the young man's rightful inheritance. He wrote:

Dear Beethoven! You are going to Vienna in fulfilment of your long frustrated wishes. The Genius of Mozart is mourning and weeping over the death of her pupil. She found a refuge but no occupation with the inexhaustible Haydn. Through him she wishes to form a union with another. With the help of unremitting effort you shall receive Mozart's spirit from Haydn's hands.

Ludwig van Beethoven was on his way.

Vienna, City of Music

Bassoonists and Blackberries

From an outpost of empire to its very heart.
Vienna, capital city of the Holy Roman Empire,
seat of the Holy Roman Emperor, formal, correct,
proper. Where wigs were powdered and properly
fitted, where gentlemen wore tailcoats, where
practically everybody who was anybody had a title.

Capital city of music, too. Where every aristocratic
family had a salon with at least one piano in it,
where the nobility vied with each other to support

this or that musician, this or that ensemble, where a particularly wealthy aristocrat might own a whole orchestra, where every night there would be musical gatherings across the city, and where concerts in the Augarten park pavilion in spring and summer would begin at 8 o'clock in the morning.

There was another, less cultural, side to Viennese life. When it was suggested to the emperor that he should authorize the construction of licensed brothels, he replied:

The walls would cost nothing, but the expense of roofing would be horrendous, since we would need to put a roof over the whole city.

Take a look at the map and you will see that Vienna is roughly in the centre of the great European land mass, bordered by the Atlantic in the west and the Urals in the east. Travellers passed through it from all directions, bringing with them their customs, their dress, their languages . . . and their music.

Only a few years before Beethoven arrived in Vienna, a traveller described seeing in the streets of Vienna:

Hungarians in their close-fitting trousers, Poles with their flowing sleeves, Armenians and Moldavians with their half-Oriental costumes, Serbians with their twisted moustaches, Greeks smoking their long-stemmed

*pipes in the coffee-houses, bearded Muslims with broad
knives in their belts, Polish Jews with their faces
bearded and their hair twisted in knots, Bohemian
peasants in their long boots, Hungarian and
Transylvanian wagoners with sheepskin greatcoats,
Croats with black tubs balanced on their heads.*

There was a fad in the final decades of the 18th
century for all things Turkish. Gone were the fears
of invasion from the east. It was 100 years or more
since the Turks last sent an army to besiege Vienna.
Now they were peaceful traders of the Ottoman
Empire with whom traders of the Habsburg Empire
did business.

The exotic musical sounds of the east
captivated Vienna. Both Mozart and Beethoven
composed Turkish marches, and Mozart
composed an entire opera set in and around a
Turkish harem!

Music was classless. All right, the salons may have
been the preserve of the aristocracy, but that did not
stop all classes enjoying it. An English music critic
who visited Vienna wrote:

*No place of refreshment, from the highest to the lowest,
is without music; bassoonists and clarinettists are as
plentiful as blackberries, and in the suburbs at every
turn one alights upon fresh carousing, fresh fiddling,
fresh illuminations.*

> *When the Turkish army besieged Vienna in 1683, legend has*
> *it that a double-agent, Georg Franz Kolschitzky, born in*
> *Poland, a merchant who had travelled in the east and who*
> *spoke fluent Turkish, slipped out of the besieged city, through*
> *the Turkish army camped at its walls, smoking and drinking*
> *with them, feeding them interesting but useless information,*
> *and getting word out to the king of Poland about Vienna's*
> *plight. Soon after the Polish king, at the head of an army,*
> *charged down the Kahlenberg Hill at the eastern end of the*
> *hills of the Vienna Woods, routing the Turks, who fled and*
> *never returned.*

But, and it's a big but, Vienna was something else
too. It was a city living in fear.

The Walls Have Ears

Look at the date Beethoven arrived in Vienna.
November 1792. What had happened in Europe
a mere three years before? Only the single most
cataclysmic event in Europe until World War One.
The French Revolution.

And what was just a matter of months away?
Only the single most genocidal event in
Europe until World War Two. The attempt in
France to obliterate an entire class. The Great Terror.

And how did it begin? With the worst act of
regicide in European history. First the King of

It was a crucial moment in European history. Had Vienna capitulated, the victorious Turkish army would have continued marching west.

Kolschitzky became an instant hero. For his bravery, the emperor offered him a reward of his choice. What did he ask for? A licence to open a new kind of drinking house in Vienna, and sole rights to the thousands of sacks of coffee beans the Turks had left behind in their tents when they fled.

Thus Vienna acquired its first café, and remains to this day the café capital of Europe.

France, Louis XVI, mounted the guillotine, followed in a matter of months by his Queen, Marie Antoinette.

And who was Marie Antoinette? (History lesson nearly over.) None other than an Austrian archduchess, youngest daughter of the great, sadly late, Empress Maria Theresa. Yes, the Queen of France, born Maria Antonia, brought up in the beautiful Schönbrunn Palace on the outskirts of Vienna, was jeered and spat at as she stood in the tumbrel, hands bound behind her back, a plain white robe on her shoulders and a simple cloth cap on her head.

To the people of France she was the detested "Austrian whore". To the Austrians she was not just one of their own, she was a Habsburg, a member of the illustrious family that ruled an empire. So what did her brother, the emperor – an imperial army at his disposal – do to rescue his sister from the murderous revolutionaries? Absolutely nothing.

You can understand why (well, maybe). In a nutshell, the emperor and his family feared they would be next. If the people of a country as civilized and traditional as France could rise up against their monarchy, what was to stop the people of Austria doing the same?

And so Vienna, sophisticated, enlightened, artistic, became a police state. From the very top word came down that no dissent whatsoever was to be tolerated. That did not just mean meetings or publications, but words too. A police state can only function if it puts in place a network of spies, a web of informers.

Suddenly, no one could be trusted. The walls had ears. Servants, chamber maids, waiters, clerks . . . everyone was a potential spy. Enjoying a coffee and a chat in any one of the numerous cafés across the city? Watch out what you say. And as everyone knew, never ever hold a private conversation in the back of a *fiacre* (the horse-drawn cabs beloved of tourists today). Your words would be on the desk of the chief of police the next morning.

And when words were dangerous, what was safe? Music. And so Vienna became Europe's capital city of music.

Drink and Be Merry

This was the Vienna that Beethoven arrived in. He was not the only Rhinelander to have sought refuge in Vienna – though the motives of others (including his brothers) were more to do with avoiding conscription. Napoleon Bonaparte had invaded and occupied the Rhineland. Europe was at war.

These Rhinelanders stuck together. In Vienna they were immediately identifiable – young men dressed more casually than the formal Viennese, and with guttural German accents that set them apart. As exiles do, they established a favourite meeting place.

Stand today in the *Neuer Markt*, one of the oldest squares in the centre of the city, towards the lower end, the ornate fountain to your left, and you will see on the corner of the alley leading through to the (now pedestrianized) *Kärntnerstrasse* a large smartly stocked bookshop. Use your imagination, and allow it to become the bustling and noisy *Schwann Inn* (Swan Inn).

A long counter near the entrance, covered in beer and wine stains, racks of already filled pipes – Beethoven would regularly smoke one with his red wine – sawdust covering warped floorboards . . . and at the back a round table that was the preserve of the Rhinelanders.

You can hear the snatches of conversation echoing down the centuries. *"What is the latest from Bonn . . .?" "French soldiers in the streets . . .?" "My father wrote that they came looking for me . . ." "I will fight for my country, but not in a French uniform . . ."* And always a wary eye out for the spy at the next table.

You can also imagine the problems Beethoven must have given his fellow Rhinelanders, as the drink took hold, his voice grew louder, his views more extreme, cupping his hand behind his ear and telling them to *Speak up! Speak up!* as his deafness took hold.

Well, not really. Beethoven was an eccentric musician. Everybody knew that. My guess is

Note to tourists. The fountain in the Neuer Markt that Beethoven knew is still there (even if the original figures are now safe and dry in the Belvedere Palace). The centrepiece of the fountain is a statue of Providence on a plinth, the figures around the low surrounding wall representing the four tributaries of the Danube in Austria. One of these tributaries is represented by a naked man propping himself up on the low wall, one leg pointing down, the other lying on top of the wall, his buttocks on full display. The sculptor, one Georg Raphael Donner, sited this figure so that its buttocks pointed straight to the front window of a patron who had withdrawn his support.

that the spies and informers soon realized
Beethoven – whatever his views – was a danger
to nobody.

*"It's that crazy musician again, the one going deaf.
No need to waste our time on him. He's no harm to
anyone."*

Virtuoso Shootout

Music, music, music. Everywhere music.
Aristocrats outdoing themselves and each other to
sponsor the latest musical sensation. And so when
young Ludwig van Beethoven arrived in the city,
determined to make his way as a *composer*, they did
not want to know. Until he sat at the piano.
Beethoven's great good fortune was that he was a
piano virtuoso unlike any they had heard in this
city of virtuosos. Give him a theme, any theme,
and – as he had proved to Mozart – he could
improvise on it spectacularly for as long as he
liked.

And how did the aristocrats amuse themselves of an
evening? What was the entertainment they loved
best? *Improvisation contests*. I like to call them
"virtuoso shootouts". It would work like this. Two
aristocrats, patrons of the arts, would each sponsor
one pianist, they would gather in a salon of the
nobility, and the two virtuosos would compete
against each other.

The first – often an outsider, so as challenger it fell to him to kick things off – would go to the piano and play a piece of his own invention, that the other chap could not possibly have heard. He would vary it, improvise on it, show off, do what he did best, then return to his seat to applause.

The second virtuoso – the local chap – would then sit at the piano and have to repeat that new theme which he had not heard before. He would then have to improvise on it, there and then, with no preparation. That done, he would then play a theme of *his* own invention, which the first chap would have to copy. And so on, and so on, an evening's entertainment in aristocratic Vienna.

When the aristocrats of the city discovered what this young man could do at the piano, they fell over themselves to sponsor him and put him up against the local talent, and one after the other Beethoven saw them off, ran them out of town.

Thus Beethoven's fame spread, and along with it a certain reputation. This was not your typical musician, smartly dressed in tailcoat and breeches, neatly powdered wig, suitably subservient and respectful in the face of old aristocracy. In fact, take one look at him and you would expect him to be a manual labourer, or coach driver, or waiter. But put him at the piano, and *well, you simply won't believe it . . . !*

Enter Daniel Steibelt, from Berlin, capital of Prussia, a typical Prussian with his militaristic bearing, ramrod erect backbone, smartly and properly dressed, haughty manner . . . and one of the finest virtuoso pianists in all Europe.

In the spring of 1800, after a *succès fou* in Prague which earned him a considerable amount of money, he came to Vienna determined to enhance his reputation. An improvisation contest was swiftly arranged, with Beethoven being sponsored by his first great patron in Vienna, Prince Karl Lichnowsky, Steibelt by another of the city's great artistic patrons, Prince Lobkowitz (later to receive the dedication of Beethoven's *Eroica Symphony*).

Although he must have been warned, Steibelt undoubtedly fell for the clumsy, careless, almost uncouth image which Beethoven projected. In fact, when he first set eyes on his opponent, he may even have thought he was the victim of a practical joke. But this was Vienna, the setting was a great artistic salon, an easy victory here would enhance Steibelt's reputation beyond words.

As challenger, outsider, it was for Steibelt to go to the piano first. When he got there, he tossed a piece of his own music on the side of the piano, sat down and began to play.

Play *what*? Would you believe, he chose the piano part of the main theme of the final movement of Beethoven's newish *Trio Opus 11*, published two years before? Shocked? So were Beethoven's supporters. So was Beethoven. I can imagine them physically restraining him as Steibelt, playing in a condescending way, in effect mocked the simple theme. (It *is* simple: it is what Beethoven goes on to do with it that is pure Beethoven.)

Beethoven sat there becoming angrier and angrier. As Steibelt finished, rising to the applause of his supporters, Beethoven lunged towards the piano. Play against Beethoven, fine; mock his music, and you pay the price.

He saw the piece of music Steibelt had tossed on the side of the piano and picked up a sheet of it, which happened to be the cello part of a quintet by Steibelt. He showed it to the audience and what do you think he then did with it? Tear it up? Good guess, but wrong. He turned it upside down! Turned it upside down and put it on the piano music stand.

With one finger Beethoven picked out the first four notes of Steibelt's music, then played the theme that followed. He began to vary it. Vary it, and improvise on it. He started to enjoy himself. He imitated Steibelt's playing, unpicked it and put it back together again. On and on he played, mocking and ridiculing Steibelt with every note.

The hapless Steibelt, realizing he was being not just outplayed but humiliated, strode from the salon, to be hastily followed by his patron, Prince Lobkowitz (as hastily as the prince's withered hip and single crutch would allow him). A few moments later Lobkowitz returned to declare that Steibelt vowed never to set foot in Vienna again as long as Beethoven lived there.

I don't need to tell you that Beethoven lived in Vienna for the rest of his life. Steibelt kept his promise: he never again returned to Vienna. And Beethoven was never again asked to take on any virtuoso. His position as Vienna's supreme piano virtuoso was established once and for all.

Those first four notes, by the way, were in time to become the motif for one of Beethoven's greatest works, the *Eroica Symphony*.

Mulaticco Lunaticco

Three years later another virtuoso came to Vienna – not, this time, a pianist, but a violinist. The luckless and ill-fated Mr George Augustus Polgreen Bridgetower. A name forgotten to history, but a name which I, with your help dear reader, shall now do my best to restore to its rightful place in musical history.

George Bridgetower was tall, slim, good-looking, with an eye for the ladies. He was a mulatto (to use

the term of the time, regarded by some today as offensive) – his father West Indian and his mother Polish. He was a brilliant virtuoso violinist. He had performed for the King and Queen at Windsor Castle, and the Prince Regent at his London residence, Carlton House.

In 1803 he came to Vienna, where on 16 April he took part in a chamber music session at the rooms of Beethoven's great friend, the violinist Ignaz Schuppanzigh. Beethoven was there and will certainly have been introduced. Bridgetower had a request to make of Beethoven, but appears to have lost his nerve, since a little later Prince Lichnowsky agreed to escort him to see Beethoven:

In order to obtain his consent to your wishes.

And just what were those wishes? The extraordinarily bold, potentially dangerous, desire that Beethoven should compose a new violin sonata for him, and dedicate it to him. The cheek of the man!

Whether it was Bridgetower's charm (unlikely), Lichnowsky's influence (also unlikely), or just that he happened to catch Beethoven in a good mood (most likely), Beethoven agreed.

More than that, when Schuppanzigh suggested that the two men perform the new piece at the inaugural concert of the summer season in the Augarten pavilion in less than a month's time, Beethoven agreed again . . .

. . . And immediately regretted it.

Schuppanzigh, by the way, was exceedingly fat, and was mercilessly teased for it by Beethoven. Beethoven even commemorated it musically. He composed a song entitled Lob auf den Dicken (In Praise of Fatness), *in which the opening line is* Schuppanzigh ist ein Lump (Schuppanzigh is a rascal), *and set it for full unaccompanied chorus and three solo male voices. I have a recording of it: in concert it lasts for 31 seconds. Who says Beethoven does not have a sense of humour?*

The date of that concert was set for 22 May, at 8 o'clock in the morning. Yes, 8 o'clock in the morning, the regular time for the summer series of concerts in the pavilion of the Augarten public park.

Beethoven quickly realized he would not be able to compose a new violin sonata in time. Surprisingly for him – and to the great benefit of musical history – instead of simply pulling out, he set about putting something together.

First of all he took the final movement intended for an earlier violin sonata (and replaced), and transferred it unaltered to the new piece. He then set about working on the first two movements.

The lethal opening bars of the first movement, involving solo double-double-stopping across all four strings by the violinist – which brings dread today to the greatest of virtuosos – Beethoven put in almost certainly because it was one of Bridgetower's party tricks. (Bridgetower had *really* got him in a good mood.)

The first movement Beethoven the perfectionist made much longer than he needed to, to match the length of the already completed third movement. He had barely sketched out the solo violin part for it, when he began work on the middle movement, which he decided to make a theme and variations (one of his favourite forms which he knew he could work on swiftly). The date of the concert was put back by two days, to the 24th, to give Beethoven a little more time.

At half past four on the morning of the concert (*yes!*) he summoned his pupil and helper Ferdinand Ries, gave him sheaves of manuscript paper and told him to copy the violin part for the first movement as quickly and neatly as he could:

"And the piano part?" "Don't worry. I'll improvise."
"But . . ." "Do as I say! Just do it!"

The second movement existed only as a scrawl, both parts set down by Beethoven on manuscript paper in his own, almost illegible, hand:

"Brischdauer will have to read his part over my shoulder." "Sir, he will never be able to . . ." "He will have to. It is the only way."

Imagine the scene. The Augarten pavilion on a sparkling spring morning, the audience made up of the city's most senior and wealthy aristocrats, the British Ambassador, guest of honour as a tribute to Bridgetower. Step forward Ludwig van Beethoven and George Bridgetower to perform a new violin sonata which Beethoven has been working on all night, which is unfinished, and of which only the final movement Bridgetower has seen before.

And, as any violinist will tell you today, it only happens to be the most difficult violin sonata Beethoven composed, and one of the most difficult any composer has ever composed.

A disaster in the making. The first thing Bridgetower did on climbing onto the platform was scan the audience for beautiful women. He was not disappointed. Princesses, countesses, duchesses, all dressed in their finest. *"If I can pull this off. If I can only pull this off . . ."*

With a mighty flourish he arced his bow high, brought it down, and dashed off the deadly double-double-stopping. Beethoven at the piano answered him, and together they played the slow opening. Then together they raced into the *Presto*.

81

In bar 18 of the *Presto* Beethoven took Bridgetower totally by surprise by playing a huge run on the piano, up the whole keyboard, down, up again to the very top, then ending on a single low C. This happened to come in a section Beethoven had marked to be repeated. At the same point in the repeat he played the same huge run.

Bridgetower, instead of carrying on, imitated the run on the violin, starting low on the G string, across all four strings to high on the E string, down again all the way to the open G string, then up to an E so high on the top string his little finger was almost off the fingerboard, and a leap to a single low C on the G string!

Beethoven gasped at the audacity of it. What did he do? Explode in anger? Storm off the stage? Knowing Beethoven, he could well have done. What he actually did was leap up from the piano stool, run across to Bridgetower, hug him, shout:

"Noch einmal, mein lieber Bursch!" [Once again, my fine fellow!]

. . . And they did it again.

For the second movement, the theme and variations, Bridgetower had no music. He had no choice but to stand behind Beethoven and sight-read from the piano part. Yet so successful was this

movement that, at the end of it, the audience immediately demanded two encores.

The final movement, since it was the only one of the three Bridgetower had seen and been able to rehearse, clinched a triumphant performance.

The audience – musically sophisticated, as all Viennese audiences of all classes were – knew they had witnessed and heard something special. Bridgetower was lionized across the City of Music.

Beethoven understood fully just how remarkable Bridgetower's playing had been, and he granted Bridgetower's request. He dedicated the sonata to him, writing on the title page:

Sonata Mulaticca Composte per il Mulatto Brischdauer, gran pazzo e conpositore Mulaticco [Mulatto sonata composed for the mulatto Bridgetower, great fool and mulatto composer]

That should be the end of the story. But alas, it was not so. Shortly after that historic performance at the Augarten, Beethoven and Bridgetower were in each other's company once again, when Bridgetower allowed his libidinous humour to get the better of him. He made an off-colour remark about a lady whom Beethoven knew.

Beethoven's mood changed in a trice. The high moralist was shocked and appalled. There and then he took the manuscript of the violin sonata away from Bridgetower, removed the dedication from it, and sent it instead to Europe's most famous violinist, one Rudolphe Kreutzer.

Despite pleading from Bridgetower, despite attempts by his friends to get him to change his mind, Beethoven was adamant. No one who could allow such words to cross his lips was to have a piece of music dedicated to him by Beethoven. Shortly after, Bridgetower left Vienna and the two men never met again.

Next time you go to hear the immortal *Kreutzer Sonata* in the concert hall, spare a thought for the man for whom it was written, who gave it its first performance, and to whom it was originally dedicated. I'd like to start a campaign to rename the *Kreutzer Sonata* the *Bridgetower Sonata*. Will you joint my campaign? I may have left it just a little late . . .

Two extraordinary details to round off this most poignant of stories. George Bridgetower died in poverty in a home for the destitute in Peckham, south London, and is buried in Kensal Green Cemetery, just off the A40 flyover, west of London, his name forgotten to history, victim of Beethoven's ability to forget friendships in an instant, to change mood in a moment.

As for Rudolphe Kreutzer, whose name will live on for ever thanks to that one great work (just as Waldstein's will), do you know what he said when he received the manuscript in Paris?

C'est la musique du diable. Impossible à jouer.
Il ne comprend pas le violon. [Devil's
music. Impossible to play. He doesn't understand the
violin.]

Rudolphe Kreutzer never once played it in public, the violin sonata that bears his name.

The People's Theatre

If you are in any doubt at all that Vienna was the City of Music, the fact that the Augarten spring and summer concerts began at 8 in the morning, and were hugely popular, should have been enough to convince you.

The Augarten pavilion is today a porcelain factory. Set into
the outside wall is a plaque commemorating the fact that
Mozart, Beethoven and Schubert all performed there.
Another musical link: buildings bordering this small
sophisticated park today house the members of the Vienna
Boys' Choir.

Yet public concerts were something of a rarity. They happened, of course, but were more often than not tied to special annual holidays or celebrations, or birthdays and namedays of the imperial royal family. There were in fact no purpose-built concert halls in this City of Music until after Beethoven's death (putting Vienna way behind London in this respect).

Nevertheless music could be heard every day of the week – in salons, restaurants, even the open air. Beethoven's *Wind and Piano Quintet Opus 16*, for example, had its first performance in a room above a café.

The two main theatres in Vienna were run by the government, and were thus known as Imperial Court Theatres. They were, as that implies, stuffy, formal, traditional. The Burgtheater, which was alongside the Hofburg Imperial Palace, was the official home of serious German language drama. The Kärntnertor theatre, so called because it stood at the bottom of the *Kärntnerstrasse* by the gate [*Tor*] set into the city wall, was the home of opera. That was interchangeable, and Beethoven staged concerts at both venues.

Go to Vienna today and you will find none of these buildings. The Burgtheater was pulled down late in the 19th century, to be replaced by its namesake in a different location. On the site where the

Kärntnertor theatre stood there stands today the five-star Sacher Hotel (more famous for creating the Sachertorte). The *Staatsoper*, the grand opera house across from the Sacher, was built long after Beethoven's time, virtually destroyed in a bombing raid right at the end of World War Two, and reopened in the fifties with a performance of . . . Beethoven's *Fidelio*.

One theatre that Beethoven did know, though, most certainly is still there today. The Theater an der Wien was the most important private theatre in Vienna. It offered (then as now) everything: spoken theatre, concerts, opera, ballet, and seasonal shows which we would today call pantomime. In Beethoven's day it stood alongside the narrow river Wien (Vienna) which flowed south to north around the eastern perimeter of the city towards the Danube. It still does today, but the river Wien has long since been covered over.

The most important geographical fact about this theatre is that – unlike the imperial theatres – it stood outside the *Bastei*, the thick wall surrounding the city that was built to keep out the Turkish invaders. Only a short distance outside, but it might as well have been 100 miles.

Leave the inner city, walk through one of the gates set into the *Bastei*, cross the stretch of green known as the *Glacis* (roughly today's *Ringstrasse*), and you were in a different world. These were the suburbs where the common people lived and traded, where it was perhaps just slightly safer to eat, drink and talk, away for the most part from the buildings of empire and the palaces of aristocrats.

Here (today as then) was the bustle of everyday life. Across the Wien from the theatre was the fruit and vegetable market. Rehearsals would echo to the sound of street sellers, windows opened in the summer would let in the pungent aroma of fruit sweating in the heat.

The leading light at the Theater an der Wien was none other than Emanuel Schikaneder, the man who owes his place in musical history to the fact that it was he, a decade or more earlier, who had commissioned *The Magic Flute* from Mozart, and who had been its first Papageno. To commemorate this he had a sculpture of Papageno placed among other figures above the main entrance (where it, and they, remain today).

That main entrance today, because of its historical worth, is on a small side street and not used. The modern main entrance and foyer are on the bustling main street.

Schikaneder's second claim to fame is that he was instrumental in securing for Beethoven an appointment as official composer at the Theater an der Wien, which brought with it a small apartment in the building into which Beethoven moved.

Schikaneder's motives were selfish: he was working on an opera libretto which he wanted Beethoven to set, and which he hoped would repeat the *succès fou* of *The Magic Flute*. This came to nothing, but Beethoven's long and very worthwhile – albeit not totally straightforward – association with The People's Theatre had begun.

Egyptian Hieroglyphics

Three months after his appointment at the Theater an der Wien, Beethoven was offered a benefit concert there – in other words, perform your own music, and after deduction of all costs and expenses you keep any profits.

What an opportunity, and Beethoven seized it. He scheduled a huge concert. He would conduct his *First Symphony* (which had already been heard in the Burgtheater). Then he would premiere no fewer than three completely new works: the *Second Symphony*, *Third Piano Concerto*, and the oratorio *Christus am Ölberge* (*Christ on the Mount of Olives*).

It was asking for trouble, and trouble was what he got. In a nutshell, a lot of the music was simply not ready. The head of music at the Theater an der

Wien, Ignaz Seyfried, has left an amusing account of how Beethoven asked him to turn the pages for the piano part in the concerto:

Heaven help me! It was easier said than done. I saw almost nothing but empty pages. At the most on one page or other a few Egyptian hieroglyphics, wholly unintelligible to me, were scribbled down to serve as clues for him. He played nearly all of the solo part from memory, since, as was so often the case, he had not had time to put it all down on paper.

Small wonder the concert did not set Vienna alight. One critic described the Oratorio as "too long, too artificial in structure, and lacking expressiveness". Another said the *Second Symphony* was less good than the first because it strives too hard to be new, and the *Piano Concerto* was not well received by the public.

When the most senior critic in the city displayed enormously good judgement in writing that the concert "confirms my long-held opinion that Beethoven in time can bring about a revolution in music like Mozart's", a reader wrote in to disagree.

Beethoven was rapidly acquiring a reputation in Vienna as an eccentric composer, writing rather odd pieces of music. They were worth a listen, if just out of interest, and his concerts were well worth attending, since you couldn't tell what eccentricity he was going to come up with next.

War!

What no one knew was that, while all that was going on, the seeds of by far the greatest of his works to date were coming to fruition in his head. He was working on a new symphony, not just unlike those that had gone before, but a symphony whose great opening chords were to change the course of musical history, none other than the *Third Symphony*, the *Eroica*.

Many years later Beethoven was having a dinner of fish (his favourite dish) with the poet Christoph Kuffner in the tavern "Zur Rose" in Nussdorf in the foothills of the Vienna Woods. The following conversation took place:

Kuffner: *Tell me frankly, which is your favourite among your symphonies?*

Beethoven: *Eh! Eh! The Eroica.*

Kuffner: *I should have guessed the C minor (Fifth).*

Beethoven: *No. The Eroica.*

But before the *Eroica* was to be heard, other events were to intervene, both personal and international, and all traumatic.

In swift succession, the Theater an der Wien was sold and brought under the umbrella of the Imperial Court Theatres (not a good idea, and it didn't last), Schikaneder was sacked, Beethoven's contract was terminated and he was forced to move out . . .

91

And, on 20 May 1804, in Paris, Napoleon Bonaparte declared himself Emperor. When news reached Vienna, Beethoven was so appalled that this man whom he admired, whom he regarded – and who, he believed, regarded *himself* – as one of the people, had done such a thing, that he scratched out the dedication to Napoleon on the title page of the *Eroica*, declaring the French ruler was:

Nothing more than a tyrant like everybody else.

Three months later both Beethoven and Schikaneder were reinstated at the Theater an der Wien, and Beethoven was able to resume work on a huge musical project that the theatre had contracted him to, namely the composition of an opera – his first.

A disaster in the making . . .

After toings and froings over the libretto, arguments with the theatre, disputes with the soloists, the date for the first performance of *Leonore* was set for 30 September 1805. Days before it, the censor banned the performance. Corrupt rulers? Prisoners allowed out into the sunlight? A woman disguised as a man rescues her husband from prison? Revolutionary and seditious, said the censor.

It took a week to get the censor to change his mind, then the truly unthinkable happened. The French

Revolutionary Army, its Commander in Chief and Emperor of his people Napoleon Bonaparte at its head, rode into Vienna and occupied the city. To add insult to injury, Napoleon took up residence in the Habsburg Emperor's summer palace at Schönbrunn. Uniformed French soldiers walked empty streets and drank in empty cafés and taverns.

The first performance of *Leonore* was now scheduled to take place on 20 November. As if the struggle to get the wretched piece performed at all had not been bad enough, now the ordinary people of Vienna, who under other circumstances could have been guaranteed to flock to *their* theatre to see a new piece of eccentricity by Beethoven, stayed away.

At the first performance, the Theater an der Wien was completely empty. Then, at subsequent performances, who made up the bulk of audience? Why, French army officers, of course. And did they like *Leonore*, with its subversive anti-authoritarian plot? Oh dear me, they did not.

The opera was doomed. Convenient though it might be, we cannot blame the fiasco entirely on the French army. *Leonore* consisted of three huge acts lacking in the necessary drama (blame the librettist Sonnleithner). Beethoven was persuaded to revise the opera completely, with a new libretto by his old friend Stephan von Breuning. In this new form, reduced to two acts, much improved, it was given again at the

Theater an der Wien in the new year (French troops having largely withdrawn from Vienna).

Success, but Beethoven knew how to turn success into disaster. He accused the theatre manager, Baron von Braun (no fan of his), of swindling him out of receipts, demanded the return of the score, stormed out of the theatre with the manuscript under his arm, and forbade any further performance of it . . .

. . . To the despair of his friends and supporters. But he knew something they did not. The opera was still not right. It was to be a further eight years before the opera was heard again, by which time it was, of course, his great masterpiece *Fidelio*.

Disaster

Yes, disaster upon disaster. No account of the life of Beethoven is complete without a report of the concert of 22 December 1808. The single most important, extraordinary – and disastrous – concert of Beethoven's entire life.

It was a long-promised and long-awaited benefit concert, and thus a showcase for Beethoven's music and a potential source of valuable income. Beethoven was in the worst possible frame of mind as the date approached, and difficult though he was to deal with, we can really hardly blame him. He had been promised this benefit concert by the city's musical bigwigs nearly a year before. It had been postponed again, and again, and again.

In the autumn of 1808, with impeccable timing, an envoy arrived in Vienna from the court of King Jerome in Westphalia offering Beethoven the job of *Kapellmeister*, and inviting him to name his salary. Beethoven was by now so utterly fed up with musical life in Vienna that he accepted.

Only the timely intervention of his greatest of all patrons, Archduke Rudolph – who with two of his wealthy aristocrat friends offered to pay Beethoven an annuity for life on the sole condition that he remain in Vienna – persuaded him to stay.

Then, finally, once and for all, he was given a firm date for his long-awaited benefit concert: 22 December. Which just happened to clash with one of the highlights of the musical calendar, a concert given by the Society of Musicians in aid of the Widows and Orphans Fund in the Burgtheater. Vienna's most senior musician, *Kapellmeister* Salieri (yes, he of *Amadeus* fame) wrote to every instrumental player of any note in Vienna, warning them that if they played for Beethoven on the 22nd, he would never work for the imperial orchestras again.

Thus it was a thoroughly motley group of musicians who gathered to rehearse with Beethoven. Rehearse what? Nothing less than two new symphonies, Nos.

5 and 6 (The *Pastoral*), a new Piano Concerto (the Fourth), two movements from the *Mass in C*, a soprano aria, and a new *Choral Fantasia* for piano, orchestra, and chorus.

It was an impossible task. The musicians knew it; Beethoven would not accept it. At the first rehearsal there was a furious row between Beethoven and the musicians. So serious that they refused to rehearse unless he went into a side room and did not interfere. Only the intervention of a couple of section leaders persuaded them to continue at all.

There was not enough time to rehearse everything, and so as the theatre filled up for the concert to begin at 6.30 pm, the potential for disaster was overwhelming. It was made all the worse by the fact that it was a bitterly cold December evening, and theatres in this era had no heating.

One can only imagine what a hash these very average musicians made of the two symphonies. The opening of the Fifth, now the most famous bars in all classical music, demands a clear beat from the conductor and a precision entry from the orchestra. One report of the time talks of the music bringing smiles to the audience. Certainly they will have laughed out loud at the bird calls in the *Pastoral*. *It's that eccentric Herr Beethoven again.*

The soprano aria was a disaster. Beethoven had engaged one of the city's foremost singers, then managed to insult her to such an extent that she refused to sing. In her place was a young girl, so frightened by what she was called on to do that she fluffed the performance completely.

In the piano concerto, Beethoven was so overwrought that he leapt up from the piano stool, knocking the candles out of the hands of the two boys standing beside him to light his score. How the audience must have loved it!

What next? Well, the entertainment was not over yet. There was one more catastrophe to come.

The final piece in the concert was to be the brand new *Choral Fantasia*, which was to begin with a solo improvisation by Beethoven on the piano, then the orchestra would come in, and in the final phase the chorus would enter.

Problem 1: There had been no time to rehearse the piece. Problem 2: Beethoven had not even had time to write out the piano part. Problem 3: The audience was by now frozen.

Seyfried and Clement, the two senior orchestra members, tried to persuade Beethoven to drop the piece completely. He refused. *Then at least drop the repeat of the second variation.* Beethoven agreed.

He took his place at the piano and began to play. Improvise, rather than play. It was music the orchestra had never heard before, so they did not know when to come in. Taking their lead from Seyfried and Clement they finally entered in chaotic fashion.

First variation. Second variation. Third variation. Except that Beethoven forgot the agreement to drop the repeat of the second variation, so he played it and the orchestra did not.

Chaos. Seyfried and Clement struggled to keep the piece on the rails, did all they could to correct things, as Beethoven played on, shouting at them as he played. Finally even he knew it was hopeless. He stopped, stormed over to the orchestra and blamed them for being a bunch of incompetents who had completely ruined the piece.

They stood their ground, threatening to walk off the stage *en masse* if Beethoven did not apologize; Seyfried and Clement tried to restore order . . .

And suddenly the audience were not cold any more. They simply could not believe what they were witnessing.

It's Beethoven! You never know what to expect!

And yet that audience had heard the first ever performance of Beethoven's *Pastoral Symphony*, and the first ever performance of the most famous symphony ever composed by anyone, Beethoven's *Fifth*.

Imagine, just imagine, if you had been there.

"I Am Deaf"

Can you begin to imagine a worse fate to befall a composer than to go deaf? There is nothing, surely, that is likely to cause a composer more anguish than to lose the one sense that should be more highly developed in him than anyone (Beethoven's words, by the way, not mine – see below).

When I first began researching into Beethoven's life, I thought he had gone to bed one night as a young man . . . and woken up the next morning deaf. It happens. Not in Beethoven's case. The first we know of any sort of problem with his hearing is a letter he wrote from Vienna to his oldest childhood friend back in Bonn, Franz Wegeler. Hardly surprising: Wegeler was now a qualified doctor, and with Bonn a comfortable 500 or so miles away there was no danger of Beethoven's secret leaking out.

In the letter, which is several pages long and begins with Beethoven bringing his old friend up to date with his musical activities, he slips almost by accident into the problems he's having with his health. But once he starts there's no stopping him. It begins with this crucial sentence:

That jealous demon, my wretched health, has put a nasty spoke in my wheel; and it amounts to this, that for the last three years my hearing has become weaker and weaker.

For the last three years . . . Beethoven dated the letter 29 June without a year, though from other things he says in the letter we can put it beyond doubt in 1801. Beethoven was thus 30 years and 6 months old when he wrote it. He was a notoriously bad time keeper and *for the last three years* is not very precise, but with an issue as important to him as this, we can give him the benefit of the doubt and safely assume that he was around 27 years of age when he first noticed that something was happening to his hearing.

This was a truly appalling time for the problems to have begun. He had been in Vienna for little under

a decade and, as we have seen, had established himself firmly in musical circles, having given a number of concerts and published several important works. There was also no shortage of wealthy aristocrats ready and willing to sponsor and commission him.

Doctor Knows Best

He explains to Wegeler that he has already been to see a number of doctors, details the treatment they have prescribed, and concludes they're all quacks and the treatments a waste of time.

I could move swiftly on here and spare you the details, but given that Beethoven is always portrayed as irritable and difficult for no apparent reason, it might be illuminating to give you an idea of just what he was going through.

First of all his hearing was not the only problem. He was suffering particularly badly from his perennial problems of colic and diarrhoea, and the doctors seemed convinced this was affecting his hearing. The first doctor, he writes in the letter to Wegeler, gave him strengthening medicines for the diarrhoea and made him wear cotton steeped in almond oil in his ears. Useless: *my deafness* [the first time he has actually used that word] *became even worse and my stomach continued to be in the same state as before.*

A second doctor, a *medical asinus*, made him sit in cold baths. One can imagine what that did to him. A more sensible doctor, he notes, made him sit in warm water from the Danube (presumably at a bath house). The result on his stomach was miraculous, but his deafness became worse still.

Enter Dr Gerhard von Vering, highly respected surgeon with a distinguished army career as regimental surgeon behind him, personal friend of the emperor, and (in years to come) overall director of all imperial hospitals during the Napoleonic wars.

> *Before we look at Dr Vering's miracle cure, a little aside. Why might Beethoven have chosen this distinguished medic? Well, one of his pupils at this time was Giulietta Guicciardi, with whom he was in love and to whom he dedicated the* Moonlight Sonata. *One of her best friends was Julie von Vering, an excellent pianist and daughter of Dr von Vering. Beethoven soon undoubtedly fell in love with Julie too, who went on to marry his best friend in Vienna (and boyhood friend from Bonn) Stephan von Breuning. Beethoven dedicated his rarely heard piano transcription of the* Violin Concerto *to Julie (the so-called* Sixth Piano Concerto). *She died tragically young, after only 11 months of marriage, possibly in childbirth.*

Beethoven, with good reason considering his reputation, had high hopes of Dr Vering. And the doctor did not disappoint. First he tackled the diarrhoea: once again warm baths in Danube water, but now with the addition of *a bottle of strengthening ingredients*. The result was miraculous. For the first time for a long time Beethoven stopped suffering from this debilitating condition.

The doctor, no doubt emboldened by this success, then prescribed pills for the colic and an infusion for the ears. The colic improved and Beethoven was able to report feeling stronger and better. Alas, he wrote: *My ears continue to hum and buzz day and night. I must confess that I lead a miserable life.*

One suspects that Beethoven would readily have sacrificed his stomach and bowel to restore his hearing. He was beginning to suspect that the doctors did not know what to do about the problem, and could not have been too heartened by Vering's classic assurance – classic in the sense that this is a doctor hedging his bets – that, as Beethoven quotes him in the letter, *My hearing will certainly improve, although my deafness may not be completely cured.*

Vering did not give up, and Beethoven stuck with him. Five months later he again wrote to Wegeler detailing Vering's latest bright idea. This was to strap the bark of the *Daphne mezereum* plant to his arms, in order to raise blisters. Lancing the blisters would cure the deafness. Given that the plant – as any self-respecting gardener knows – is, despite its fragrant and attractive flower, highly poisonous, causing swelling of lips and tongue, thirst, difficulty of swallowing, nausea, vomiting, internal bleeding with bloody diarrhoea, weakness, and coma, it is not entirely surprising Beethoven found it an extremely unpleasant treatment. Not least because during the several days it took for the bark to draw, he could not freely use his arms (unfortunate for a pianist), and was also in great pain.

Beethoven was losing patience with Vering, and took up Wegeler's suggestion that he see a friend of his, Dr Johann Schmidt, who was pioneering the latest medical craze in Vienna, galvanism, which, it was said, had cured a man who had been deaf for seven years.

Peace and Quiet

We do not know for sure that Schmidt tried galvanism on Beethoven. Is seems unlikely – it would surely be documented, or Beethoven would have told Wegeler or other friends about it, given that it is a somewhat extreme treatment, involving the passing of an electrical current through a muscle to force it to contract. If he did, it did not work.

But Beethoven was not put off. Why should he be? Schmidt adored music and was an accomplished violinist whose daughter played the piano. More to the point, he made the first truly sensible suggestion any doctor had made: get away from Vienna, the noise and dust and bustle of the city; go and stay in the countryside for a prolonged period, and give your ears a good rest.

It worked. Well, it worked, sort of. He spent the summer of 1802 – no fewer than five months from May to October – in the small village of Heiligenstadt, a couple of hours' carriage ride north of Vienna (today a quiet suburb just a few stops from the city centre on the *Untergrundbahn*). His hearing certainly did not improve; in fact it probably continued to deteriorate, though Beethoven does not specifically say that.

But in two very important respects the stay was a success. First of all, Beethoven was able to work uninterrupted, composing a huge set of piano variations and putting the finishing touches to his *Symphony No. 2*. Second – and the importance of this is impossible to overstate – for the first time he came to terms with his deafness. In other words, he accepted it. Let's face it, he had known it all along. His hearing was going to continue to deteriorate, whatever the doctors did. They were all quacks; what did they know? There was no cure. He was, sooner or later, going to become stone deaf.

It hit him, uncompromisingly, full on, unavoidably, while he was out walking in the countryside around

Heiligenstadt with his young friend and helper, Ferdinand Ries [*see **The Cast List**]*. Ries, unwittingly putting both feet in it, stopped and commented on the beautiful sound of a shepherd's pipe floating on the still summer air. Beethoven could not hear it. The game was up. He really was deaf and he knew and accepted now that it was incurable.

On 6 October Beethoven sat at the table in his Heiligenstadt lodgings, no doubt fortified himself with a carafe of rough local red wine, dipped his quill in the inkpot, and wrote the most important manuscript he ever wrote that was not in the form of musical notes. It was, in fact, at the age of just 31 years and 10 months, his Last Will and Testament. It is flowery and melodramatic, but given the magnitude of his despair, we can surely forgive him. Here are the most important passages:

Oh, all you people who think and say that I am hostile to you, or that I am stubborn, or that I hate mankind, you do not realise the wrong that you do me. You think you understand, but you do not know the secret cause of my seeming that way . . . For the last six years I have suffered from a terrible condition, made worse by stupid doctors, yet hoping from one year to the next that it would improve, but finally realising that I'd been deceived, that I would have to accept the prospect of a lasting malady . . . I am deaf . . . Oh God, how could I possibly explain that I was deficient in the one sense that should have been more highly developed in me than anyone, a sense that I once possessed to perfection, to an extent that few in my profession do or ever have? . . . For me there can be no enjoyment in other men's company, no stimulating conversations or exchange of ideas. I must be totally alone . . . I must live like an exile . . . Only a little more and I would even have ended my life. Only my *art, that is all that held me back . . .*

Only a little more and I would even have ended my life . . . The *Heiligenstadt Testament*, as it is known, is not a suicide note. But what I believe Beethoven is doing here is reserving the right to himself to end his life at any time he decides, and the obvious moment will be when he can no longer hear his own music.

It is a manifestation of his courage and determination that when that time came, he did not end his life. Not only that, but as his deafness became more and more profound, so his compositions became all the greater. One of the great miracles of art.

Heiligenstadt was the turning point. He continued to see doctors for the rest of his life, taking pleasure in sacking them summarily. He allowed them to treat the colic and diarrhoea which pursued him throughout his life, but he never took any notice of advice about his deafness again. He knew more about it than they did.

That priceless document, the Heiligenstadt Testament, *passed into the hands of Beethoven's sister-in-law soon after his death. Johanna, ever short of money, asked Franz Liszt, no less, to try to sell it on her behalf in England. He succeeded, but the price did not match the 50 guineas that Johanna had demanded. Liszt made up the difference out of his own pocket.*

In September 1888 it was, thankfully, bequeathed to the Hamburg City Library. It is today preserved intact at the Staats- und Universitätsbibliothek (State and University Library) *in Hamburg.*

"Try This, Herr Beethoven"

One person he *did* listen to was a rather eccentric chap whose name has gone down in musical history as the inventor of the metronome, Johann Nepomuk Mälzel. "Inventor" is the right word; that is what he did, and what he specialized in was mechanical musical instruments – of which the most famous was his Panharmonicon, a machine which could produce the sounds of a full orchestra.

In around 1812 Beethoven became very friendly with Mälzel, frequently visiting his workshop. Why? Because Mälzel made him an offer he simply could not refuse.

He promised he could improve Beethoven's hearing – not cure it medically, but improve it, by amplifying the sound going into Beethoven's ears. One can imagine this enthusiastic boffin explaining about sound and how it penetrates the ears and enters the skull, and Beethoven shutting him up and telling him to get to the point.

Get to the point he did, by making no fewer than four different copper ear trumpets for Beethoven to try. One was long, with an open cylinder at the speaking end and a curved neck collar at the other to hold the contraption in place. Another was also long, with a closed cylinder with holes like a colander at the speaking end and no collar. The third was short and small with a curved neck collar. The fourth was a little longer, slightly curved, no collar, rather like a hunting horn.

It was this fourth one – the simplest in design and most comfortable to use – that worked best. Beethoven was overjoyed. He could hear again! Prints of the time show Beethoven concentrating hard, holding the trumpet to his ear, while someone speaks into the other end.

But the euphoria did not last, for the very simple reason that as his hearing deteriorated, the trumpet became less effective. Finally – after around eight to 10 years (a substantial time) – he threw it away, recognizing his deafness was now so profound nothing could be done to help it.

Musical history owes Mälzel a debt, not just for the metronome, but for persuading Beethoven to produce one of his quirkiest compositions. On 21 June 1813 the Duke of Wellington secured a famous victory against the French at the Battle of Vitoria in northern Spain. There were huge celebrations in Vienna, which had twice been occupied by Napoleon Bonaparte. Mälzel persuaded Beethoven to compose a piece of music for his Panharmonicon to celebrate the British victory. Beethoven agreed, and the result was the "Battle Symphony" Opus 91.

Yes, you read it right. Beethoven composed his Battle Symphony *or, to give it its full title,* Wellington's Sieg oder die Schlacht bei Vitoria [Wellington's Victory or the Battle

Resignation

Everyone knows the *Emperor Piano Concerto*, but it is instructive to note that it was Beethoven's last piano concerto, and he composed it as early as 1809 when he was just 38.

The Emperor *is the one with that famous opening where the soloist has to play those furious opening runs right at the beginning, after just a single chord from the orchestra, before he or she has had time to hear the sound of the orchestra, hear the sound of the piano, gauge the tempo the conductor has set, gauge the mood of the audience . . . and then sit doing nothing for several minutes. Beethoven did not believe in making it easy.*

of Vitoria] *for a mechanical orchestra! How on earth did Mälzel persuade this most serious-minded and difficult of composers to do such a thing? We do not know, but my theory is that Beethoven did it out of gratitude for the ear trumpets that did so much to help his hearing.*

By the way, we can never know exactly what Mälzel's fabulous Panharmonicon looked like. (We can guess that it was a large box-like construction with pipes, valves, pedals, knobs, bells and whistles.) In 1838, on a visit to the US and the Caribbean, Mälzel was on board a brig sailing from Havana to Philadelphia. The ship went down, taking Mälzel and his Panharmonicon with it.

Why, then, not another piano concerto in the remaining 18 years of his life, all the more remarkable since the piano was *his* instrument, and he frequently performed his own concertos (as Mozart had done) to much acclaim and considerable remuneration?

We cannot know for certain, but the answer surely has to be that he realized his deafness was becoming so severe he would no longer be able to perform his own works in public – at least, not major works with orchestral accompaniment.

What about smaller works? The answer was not long in coming. On 11 April 1814 Beethoven was due to perform his new *Piano Trio Opus 97*, known to us today as the *Archduke Trio*, in the concert hall of the grand hotel *zum Römischen Kaiser* (*at the Holy Roman Emperor*). Rehearsals were a disaster.

A friend of Beethoven's who attended reported that:

In the first place the piano was out of tune, which didn't matter to Beethoven since he couldn't hear it. Secondly, because of his deafness there was scarcely anything left of the artist who formerly had been so greatly admired. In forte *passages the poor deaf man pounded on the keys till the strings jangled, and in* piano *passages he played so softly that whole groups of notes were left out, so that the music was unintelligible . . . It is a great misfortune for anyone to be deaf, but how can a musician endure it without giving in to despair? At last I could fully understand Beethoven's continual melancholy.*

It is highly likely that Beethoven's violinist friend, Ignaz Schuppanzigh, tried to talk him out of playing the piano part in performance, and we know that Beethoven's formidable pupil Carl Czerny was ready to stand in.

If you've ever taken piano lessons, the name Czerny should strike dread into your stomach. All those hundreds of piano exercises. Yes, it was the same Czerny who was Beethoven's outstanding pupil, and who, after Beethoven's death, was able to perform each of the 32 piano sonatas from memory.

But Beethoven insisted on playing, and the performance was – predictably – embarrassing. Beethoven simply could not hear the violin and cello. He came in at the wrong places, he even played wrong notes. Unheard of for such a virtuoso.

Beethoven had tried; he knew he had failed. He tried again with the same piece a few weeks later, and failed again.

As if in a final attempt to convince himself that it was not yet all over, at the beginning of the following year he started work on a sixth piano concerto. It was not to be. He abandoned work on it in the spring.

As far as we know, Beethoven never performed in public again. His days as a virtuoso were over. From now on he was just a composer.

Acceptance

Just a composer. It is possible to become too maudlin about all this. Of course his deafness was a disaster for him, but we know that Beethoven hated performing – particularly for ignorant aristocrats whom he would often mock as he played. The end of his performing career meant he could concentrate now on composing, without the distraction of arranging concerts – and what extraordinary works he now blessed us with!

In this era, if a composer was told he could give a benefit concert – meaning he could keep all the profits after expenses had been taken – he had to do all the organizing. He had to decide on the programme (the easy bit), assemble the orchestra, arrange rehearsals, organize publicity in the musical press, print and distribute posters, even set ticket prices and sell them from his own home!

It is in the final period of Beethoven's life that we have the most profound works – the *Hammerklavier Piano Sonata, Missa Solemnis, Late String Quartets, Piano Sonatas Opuses 109, 110, 111.*

Not to mention one of the best-known compositions of all time.

Beethoven's *Ninth Symphony* (nicknamed the *Choral*) is, of course, Beethoven's final symphony; and just as Mozart's final symphony, the *Jupiter*, broke the mould so that it seemed impossible for anything to follow it, the same and more can be said about Beethoven's *Ninth*. (Interesting that neither composer saw it that way. Mozart composed the *Jupiter* more than three years before he died, and a longer life would undoubtedly have produced more symphonies. Beethoven was working on sketches for his tenth symphony when he died.)

The sophisticated Viennese concert-going public who attended the premiere of Beethoven's *Ninth* on

7 May 1824 knew the moment they heard it just how important and original a work this was. What makes it all the more remarkable is how near this glorious work came to not being performed at all [see *A New Flower Glows*, *Chapter 8*].

The $64,000 Question

What caused Beethoven's deafness? I believe that is the biggest medical mystery in the history of art. Of all the questions I have been asked over all the years about Beethoven, that is the one I am asked most.

There is a simple answer: we do not know. That is of course not an answer. As for the question, well, it was asked by doctors, friends and family in Beethoven's own lifetime, and has been asked by countless medical experts ever since. Not that there is any shortage of answers; on the contrary, each new generation seems to come up with a new explanation.

And we *still* do not know. But do not despair. One day we will know; it's just that it may not be in my lifetime or yours. More on that in a moment. For now, here are the theories and where we stand on the issue today. (Most of what follows is in the negative – nos, nots, nevers, didn't, hadn't, and so on. It's so much easier to say what was not the case than what was.)

First of all, Beethoven (as we have seen in earlier chapters) came from a family of musicians in the employ of the local prince, and there is no mention that either his father or grandfather had hearing problems (which there surely would have been, had it been the case). Nor is there any evidence of deafness on his mother's side, or concerning either of his brothers.

If we assume that Beethoven was the first in his family to have trouble with his hearing, then something must have happened to cause it. (I know that's stating the obvious, but there is so much we *don't* know, that it is worth stating everything we *do* know, or that must be the case.) That is reinforced by the fact that the problem did not start until his late twenties, which makes some kind of congenital disorder highly unlikely.

In the decades following his death, researchers were pretty sure they knew the answer. It was that curse of the 19th century, syphilis. We can now state categorically that Beethoven did not have syphilis. First of all, syphilis affects the whole system: Beethoven showed none of the other signs associated with it. Second, when strands of his hair were recently analysed [see *The Last Master*, *Chapter 10*], it was found that there were no traces of mercury in his body when he died: mercury was the standard treatment for syphilis. I know you cannot prove a negative, but Beethoven did *not* have syphilis. Believe me.

In the 20th century, as medical research advanced, there seemed to be a new diagnosis every time the wind changed. Typhoid fever, kidney stones, Crohn's disease, hepatitis, Paget's disease, jaundice, rheumatic fever, sarcoidosis, pancreatitis, and (still) syphilis, were all put forward as causes of Beethoven's deafness. You will find arguments for and against each of the above, but none is conclusive.

In the late 19th century one of the most respected Beethoven scholars related how Beethoven had told the English pianist Charles Neate that he had once been so angry that he had hurled himself to the ground in a rage, and when he got up again he found he was deaf, and had been deaf ever since. A likely story.

Two friends who knew Beethoven well both reported that he suffered from *typhus* as an adolescent, and from that moment his hearing problems began. One, a childhood friend, was writing 60 years after the event; the other, who did not meet Beethoven until years later, was writing 20 years after events he did not witness. If they were right, why did the trouble not begin for around another 10 or so years? And the word *typhus* in German translates more accurately today as *typhoid fever*. See what I mean?

119

Here is a possible explanation. We know that some time in his mid-twenties Beethoven became very ill. In May 1797 he wrote to Wegeler: *I am well and I am pleased to say my health is steadily improving*. A friend said Beethoven contracted a fever after getting soaked and hot during a long walk in the rain, then sitting down immediately to work and becoming thoroughly chilled. Another description has him returning hot and wet from a walk in the rain, then stripping to the waist and standing in front of an open window to cool down.

What was he ill with? We do not know. Whatever it was, could it have affected his hearing? Possibly.

Now here is probably the most extraordinary element of this extraordinary story. Beethoven's doctors, as I have already said, were as keen then as we are now to establish what caused Beethoven's deafness. And so when they carried out the post mortem on him, they sawed through the skull on the forehead below the hairline and removed the auditory bones. These were placed in a large sealed glass jar filled with preserving fluid and given to the mortuary orderly.

The jar, after a long time, possibly years, disappeared.

We'll Know One Day

Do not despair. Modern science will come to our rescue. We *will* know one day; it might be

tomorrow, it might not be for many years yet. It all depends on just how fast science progresses.

By the way, even if that glass jar had survived, it is unlikely to have revealed much. In order to examine the inner ear you need a microscope. This was 1827, and the world was to move well into a new century before such equipment was available. And the chances of that jar surviving intact, with its contents undisturbed, for another 100 years or more are pretty small.

There was a rumour in Vienna that the mortuary orderly, one Anton Dotter, sold the auditory bones to a foreign physician. Much later there was another rumour that the bones ended up in London and were destroyed during a German bombing attack during World War Two.

The day after Beethoven's death, his body still on the deathbed, numerous friends – and some who merely claimed to be – came to pay their respects . . . and to cut off a lock of Beethoven's hair to preserve as a memento. Little did they know the favour they were doing to future generations.

If you had told them that one day, in around 200 years or a little less, scientists would be able to analyze those strands of hair and learn much about Beethoven's physical makeup, they would no doubt have taken you for a fool.

121

Similarly, when those doctors sawed across the front of Beethoven's forehead, they cannot have imagined that fragments of his skull that splintered off and were kept, again as a memento, would surface almost two centuries later and once again become a treasure trove for learning about Beethoven's health and genetic makeup.

It's all down to those three magic letters which have transformed science in the early 21st century: DNA.

More on those strands of hair, and fragments of skull, in Chapter 10.

For now, all that need be said is this. If science has moved that far in two centuries, where might it be in two centuries from now? And for you and me, and Beethoven lovers all, I can state with absolute certainty – even if you and I are long gone before it happens – that one day those precious relics will enable scientists to solve the greatest mystery of the most famous deaf person who ever lived.

Beethoven's Women

An Eye for the Ladies

Beethoven was a lifelong bachelor. Beethoven never married.

Yes, I know that's the same thing said two different ways, but I've done it on purpose. If the second most common question I am asked about Beethoven (after *What caused his deafness?*) is *How old was he when he died?* then the third most common is *Did he ever marry?* It's as if there's an assumption that he did. There's even a (quite good) joke (one of the very, very few) about Beethoven, of which the punch line is spoken by his wife. (No I won't. It has to be heard, not read.)

Given that he never married, given that the usual image of him is of an angry, difficult man, with unkempt clothes, hair in disarray, scowling face, utterly absorbed in his music, it is tempting to say not only that he had no time for women, that he regarded them as a distraction, but that even possibly he disliked them. One notorious book published in the US in the 1950s set out to show that he was a woman-hating homosexual. He was neither a woman-hater nor a homosexual.

Certainly not if we are to believe his friend and helper Ferdinand Ries, who for many years lived more closely to Beethoven and knew him better than any other individual.

He tells an illuminating story, which seems to me to encapsulate Beethoven's behaviour towards women. We already know from his (probable) attempt to extract more than a polite kiss from Eleonore von Breuning that he was awkward with women. Whatever he did, we know she was offended. Even if we put it down to the gaucheness of an inexperienced young man, Ries's story shows he did not improve with age.

We do not know the year, but it is likely to have taken place in the autumn of 1808, when

Beethoven was 37 years of age. He and Ries were in
Baden, the spa town south of Vienna. Ries was due
to have an evening lesson with his master, went to
the house where he was staying, and found him
sitting on the sofa alongside a beautiful young
woman. Ries deduced from the manner of them
both that Beethoven had somehow offended the
woman and was trying to make amends. Realizing
he was intruding, he turned to leave immediately,
but Beethoven stopped him:

*Ries, sit down and play for a while! . . . Something
romantic! . . . Now something melancholy! . . .
Something passionate! . . .*

Ries, a very capable pianist, played several of
Beethoven's own pieces, connecting them with
passages of his own. Suddenly Beethoven jumped
up:

Why, those are all things that I have written!

Ries is too discreet and respectful to go into detail,
but one can assume Beethoven turned to the
woman with an air of some triumph expecting her
to be suitably impressed. She is likely to have smiled
politely but said little more, because shortly
afterwards, Ries says, she stood up and left.

Ries asked Beethoven who she was, and was greatly
surprised when he said he did not know. She had

apparently come to the house because she had heard
he was there and wanted to meet him. Ries was
even more surprised when Beethoven suggested they
leave the house immediately and follow her.

It was a moonlit night, and they could see her in
the distance. They followed her, but then she
suddenly disappeared and they lost her. They
continued walking for another hour and a half or
more in the valley on the edge of the town, talking
about all kinds of things. When they parted,
Beethoven said:

I must find out who she is and you must help me.

Some considerable time later Ries met the woman
in question in Vienna and ascertained that she was
the mistress of a foreign prince. When he relayed
the news to Beethoven, he showed no interest at all,
apparently behaving as if the incident had never
happened and the woman never existed.

Typical Beethoven. Voraciously interested in the
woman, flattered by her interest in him, managing
unwittingly to offend her, following her in a way
which today we might find a little worrying (it's not
quite stalking, but it's not far off), then completely
forgetting the whole episode.

When Beethoven admired women, he was content
to do so from afar. Ries left Vienna for London not

long after the incident in Baden and married an English woman renowned for her beauty. In numerous letters to him over the ensuing years, Beethoven referred to the beauty of Ries's wife, the physical distance between them allowing him to be as bold as he liked:

I hear your wife is beautiful, I must kiss her now merely in my mind, but I hope to have that pleasure in person next winter . . . In the spring of next year I shall be coming to London in order to kiss your wife . . . Regarding your marriage, you will always find in me an opposition *to you and a* proposition *for your wife . . . The only reward I shall accept is a kiss from your wife which I am to receive from her in London.*

Poor Beethoven. He never came to London, and he never met the beautiful Mrs Ries.

Queen of the Night

Try insulting a woman and see if you can come up with anything better (worse) than this:

The notorious whore . . . Last night that Queen of the Night *was at the Artists' Ball until 3 a.m. exposing not only her mental but also* her bodily nakedness – *it was whispered that she was willing to hire herself for 20 gulden! Oh horrible!*

All the more insulting when you consider that it is almost certainly untrue, given that no one else at the Artists' Ball reported anything of the kind going on.

So who was the object of Beethoven's venom? Who was he comparing to Mozart's arch villainess in *The Magic Flute*? Someone he knew personally, or by repute? The wife or lover of a friend or fellow musician? No. She was none other than his very own sister-in-law, mother of his adored nephew Karl.

Her name was Johanna van Beethoven (*née* Reiss), and the relationship Beethoven had with her was the most complicated, contradictory, irrational, illogical he ever had with any woman. (Should you doubt it, the next chapter detailing the court case he waged against her will convince you.)

To give Beethoven the very smallest credit for his vicious words about her, Johanna was a woman with a certain reputation. In Beethoven's eyes there was no greater evidence of this than the fact that she was visibly pregnant when his brother married her. Beethoven did everything he could to dissuade Carl from marrying her, then after the marriage everything he could to persuade Carl that she was a deeply immoral woman and he should exclude her totally from the upbringing of their son.

Johanna's tarnished image was not based solely on her reputation for being liberal with her favours. As a teenager she had accused the family maid of stealing something she had herself taken. The case went to court, she was forced to admit her dishonesty, and was fortunate no action was taken against her.

This was sadly not just a case of teenage folly. When she was 25 years of age, married and a mother, Johanna did something so stupid it beggars belief. It was to haunt her, and provide a stick for her brother-in-law to beat her with, for years to come.

A friend gave her a multi-stringed pearl necklace to sell on commission. Instead Johanna sold some of the strings privately, and kept others. She then faked a burglary at her house and reported the strings stolen. It took the police five minutes to establish what had happened. Johanna was arrested, charged, convicted of embezzlement and sentenced to one year's imprisonment – a harsh punishment that shocked all involved. On appeal it was reduced to two months' imprisonment, then reduced again to one month's detention in police cells, and finally reduced to one month's house arrest which was not enforced.

But the damage was done. Never mind her already colourful reputation, Johanna – mother of the boy who was to prove to be the only Beethoven of the next generation – had a criminal record. It was the main plank of Beethoven's legal action against her after his brother, her husband, the father of her child, died, and he fought her for custody of the boy. (A case with such an impact on Beethoven's life it deserves, and will get, a chapter on its own.)

To give Beethoven just an ounce more credit, when he tried to convince his brother he was making a mistake in marrying Johanna, and the marriage was destined to be unhappy, he was not entirely wrong. The *chain of sorrows* that made up the marriage of Beethoven's own mother was certainly passed on to the next generation, though the blame cannot be laid entirely at Johanna's door.

Johanna may have been a flighty woman, but there is no evidence she was a difficult wife or uncaring mother. There was the small matter of the conviction for embezzlement, true, but as far as we know she never transgressed again.

Carl van Beethoven, by way of contrast, was a thoroughly mean piece of work. A failed musician, for a time he ran his brother's business affairs and once tried to pass off some of his own pathetic attempts at composition as being by his famous brother, leading – not unnaturally – to Beethoven refusing to allow Carl to have anything more to do with his publishers or patrons. He eventually secured a lowly position as clerk in a government department, earning barely enough to keep his wife and young son.

He was almost certainly a wife-beater, and definitely violent. Johanna's future daughter-in-law reported that on one occasion, during a furious row, Carl had stabbed his wife through the hand with a table knife, and that Johanna still bore the scar as an old lady.

After Carl's early death from consumption (like his mother), Johanna did little to improve her reputation – though after living for years with a violent good-for-nothing husband, and suffering dreadful insults from her famous brother-in-law, we should perhaps not judge her too harshly. She became pregnant four years later and named the baby Ludovica, the female form of Ludwig (psychoanalysts take note). She told the man she was having an affair with that he was the father, extracting a generous paternity allowance from him. In fact (according to Beethoven's other brother) the child's true father was a student lodger to whom she had rented out a room in her house.

So what are we to make of Beethoven's relationship with his sister-in-law? Seen through his eyes, she was the mother of Karl, the boy who would carry the cherished and sacred name of *Beethoven* forward. But as a wicked and immoral woman, she must be kept out of the boy's future at all costs. The fact that the boy was of her flesh and blood was entirely irrelevant.

All highly logical and rational, but utterly insensitive and unfeeling. Could this be, then, a case of a man who falls in love with a woman he knows to be promiscuous and immoral, despises himself for it, subconsciously blames the woman, and transfers all his self-loathing and disgust on to her?

Gulp! That really is one for the psychoanalysts. Just as it is difficult, and quite possibly misleading, to use modern medicine to try to diagnose Beethoven's illnesses, so it is just as dangerous to try to understand this relationship in any depth without being able to put him on a psychiatrist's couch.

Inevitably there were rumours that his attitude towards Johanna might be caused by deeper, suppressed feelings. Both were aware of these whisperings. In a conversation book (notebooks used by Beethoven once his deafness had taken hold) one of his friends reports Johanna as saying Beethoven was in love with her, and Beethoven himself later wrote in a letter of "the well-worn complaints of Frau Beethoven about me, that I was supposed to be in love with her, etc, and more rubbish of that kind".

This much we can say. In later life there is evidence Beethoven at least partially regretted his harshness towards Johanna – once he had come to the woeful realization that Karl really was an average, mediocre individual, without the slightest amount of musical talent. He inquired from friends about her welfare, and forwarded some money to her (at arm's length).

What is truly remarkable about Johanna van Beethoven is that, although she survived her difficult and combative brother-in-law by more than 40 years, although he had done everything in his power to blacken her name, although he had dragged her through the courts to wrest control of her son from her, she never – as far as I can ascertain – in all that time wrote or said a single word against him.

Johanna, a widow for 52 years, and living in constant poverty, died in her early 80s, having outlived her only son by almost 10 years. It was an undoubtedly sad life, and she must often have rued the day when she first came into contact with the Beethovens. She will certainly have taken many a secret about her world-famous brother-in-law to the grave. Had she, and he, lived in a different era, she could have made a fortune from a kiss-and-tell exposé.

A "Dear, Enchanting Girl"

Quite a relief to be on firmer – or at least less complicated – psychological ground with the next of Beethoven's women, who is perhaps the woman he came closer than any other to marrying.

Create this picture in your mind. A cold November day in Vienna, Beethoven in despair over the onset of deafness. It is only five months since he has first revealed a problem in that searing letter to his old friend Dr Franz Wegeler in Bonn. Now, no doubt fortified with a carafe, he picks up the pen again, pouring out all his misery, the hopeless remedies he is prescribed, the asinine doctors, a new treatment he has heard of called *galvanism . . .*

Then, all of a sudden, without even a paragraph break, this:

I seem to be a misanthrope but actually I am not at all. This change has been brought about by a dear enchanting girl who loves me and whom I love. After two years I am again enjoying a few blissful moments, and for the first time I feel that marriage might bring me happiness.

The girl in question really was just a girl, a mere 16 years of age, pretty, lively, from a titled family. Her name was Countess Giulietta Guicciardi, known to friends and family as Julie, and Beethoven, at the request of her parents, had taken her on as a pupil.

It's easy to be a little cynical about those words *who loves me and whom I love.* From Julie's perspective

first, she will no doubt have been hugely impressed, dazzled even, to find herself being taught by a man famous in Vienna, a virtuoso pianist without parallel in the city, composer already of a symphony, three piano concertos, a set of string quartets, and several other chamber works. But *love*? From Beethoven's point of view, he finds himself in the same room, sitting alongside a vivacious girl with an infectious laugh, who (let us speculate) teases him fearlessly, touches his arm, forces him to laugh with her. But he is almost double her age, knows he is losing his hearing. Is a match really possible?

Well, yes. It appears love really was in the air. To such an extent that when Beethoven proposed marriage to Julie, she accepted. At about the same time he presented her with a new piano sonata he had composed. It could well have been an engagement present.

Then it all went wrong. Julie's father refused to allow the match, pointing out to his daughter that Beethoven had little money, no permanent job (many a musician's lot then, as now!), and was losing his hearing, not exactly a minor affliction for a musician. That's putting it tactfully. He probably said: *You want to marry **who**? Have you completely lost your mind? A deaf musician? You want to marry a **deaf musician**? Over my dead body!*

That was that. Julie went on to marry a mediocre musician by the name of Count Gallenberg, who secured employment in Italy where they lived for the next 18 years.

We do not know exactly how Beethoven reacted to the rejection, but if we are to believe his own account he got over it and moved on. That account came many years later in a Conversation Book. Quite why Beethoven chose to write his words (when most of the conversations in these books naturally carry only half of what was said, since Beethoven spoke his replies), and quite what made him decide to write in (appalling) French, we cannot know. But this is what he wrote:

Elle est née Guicciardi . . . avant de l'Italie et elle cherchait moi pleurant, mais je la meprisois [Her maiden name was Guicciardi . . . before going to Italy she came to see me in tears, but I rejected her]

What might have occasioned this uncomfortable scene? We do not know, but with a journalist's excitement I can reveal some exclusive information which, as far as I know, has never been published before. Restrain your impatience. All is revealed, along with other exclusive information, in *Chapter 10, The Last Master.*

Remember I said Beethoven dedicated a piano sonata to Julie? It was none other than the Arbour Sonata. *Ring a bell? I didn't think so. That was just the early title. Beethoven changed it to* Sonata quasi una Fantasia, *the title under which it was published. Still no bells?*

Right, brace yourself. Long after Beethoven's death, a music critic heard this sonata being performed and compared the first movement to the moon setting over Lake Lucerne, *and so we have . . . The* Moonlight Sonata. *Thus Beethoven's lost love, Giulietta Guicciardi, has achieved immortality.*

"For Therese"

Not many years later Beethoven was head over heels in love again, and once again he had ideas above his station. Therese Malfatti may have been described as *a flighty lady who treated everything in life light-heartedly*, but she was the daughter of a wealthy merchant of Italian extraction who owned a large house on the fashionable *Kärntnerstrasse* right in the centre of Vienna, and a portrait of her shows an elegant lady dressed to the nines in a flowing dress and tall ornate height-of-fashion hat.

Age was once again a potential problem. This time Beethoven was more than double Therese's age: he was 39, she was 18. There was an added problem which made this very different to the earlier romance with Julie. Therese was not in the least bit interested in a relationship with Beethoven.

He did not allow that simple impediment to deter him. He smartened himself up, asking the young musician acting as his assistant (who first introduced him to Therese and happened to be engaged to Therese's sister) to buy cloth for new shirts to be made up, half a dozen neckties and some new handkerchiefs.

He also wrote to Wegeler back in Bonn asking for his baptismal certificate to be forwarded to him in Vienna (cautioning him not muddle him up with his elder brother, Ludwig, who had lived for just a week).

Marriage was clearly on Beethoven's mind. How should he set about his task of wooing and winning Therese? For a man of his talents and reputation, simple. Compose a piece of music for her, dedicate it to her, take it to her house, meet, flatter and cajole her parents, present the piece to Therese, play it for her, and announce his intentions.

Not that simple, given the fact that Therese herself was not to be wooed. But for a man of Beethoven's social graces, impossible. We can piece together what happened from letters both he and his assistant wrote.

He duly turned up at the Malfatti residence, where we can imagine that the trio of Signor

Malfatti, his wife and daughter, sitting
frostily, received him. Signor Malfatti
offered Beethoven a richly concocted punch to
drink. The conversation loosened slightly, and
more drink was poured. Therese's parents
then withdrew, leaving their daughter to break
the bad news to Beethoven, no doubt promising
they would be in the next room should she
need them.

Beethoven, by now drunk, misread the whole
scene and made a lunge for Therese. She
screamed, the parents came rushing in, and
Beethoven was swiftly shown the door. Signor
Malfatti refused to allow Beethoven to set foot
inside his house again.

End of romance. Beethoven felt the hurt deeply. He
wrote to his assistant:

*Am I then nothing more than your musician or
musician to the others?*

And to Therese herself:

*Work out what I mean for yourself, but don't let
the punch try to help you . . . When you think of
me, think of me cheerfully — and do forget the wild
goings-on.*

Beethoven had been unlucky in love again.

And that piece of music he had composed for Therese?
None other than Bagatelle WoO 59. *That familiar sound*
of no bells ringing? Then, for a second time, brace yourself.
The manuscript (sadly now lost) was found in Therese's
effects when she died more than 40 years later. At the top of
the title page was a handwritten dedication from Beethoven
to Therese. Sixteen years after that it was published. On
the title page of the published manuscript the dedication
read:

> *Für Elise am 27 April zu Erinnerung an*
> *L. v. Bthvn [For Elise on 27 April as a*
> *memento of L. v. Bthvn]*

A publisher's simple error, confusing Therese for Elise? Or
Beethoven's poor handwriting leading to the mix-up of

"My Angel, My All, My Very Self"

So we come to the big one. If the cause of
Beethoven's deafness is the greatest unsolved
mystery of his life, the identity of the one
woman we know he had an affair with runs it
pretty close. All the women mentioned in
this chapter so far, and many more, have been
named as the woman in question. But still the
debate goes on.

That debate began in the days immediately
following's Beethoven's death among his family and
close colleagues, to be taken up later by academics,
musicologists, historians, novelists, filmmakers.

140

names? Or could Therese have been known by the name Elise? We do not know, but the timing of the composition, and the fact that it was in Therese's possession for the rest of her life, puts it beyond doubt that she was the dedicatee of the piece.

What piece? Für Elise, *of course, the best-known piece of piano music Beethoven ever composed, the best-known piece of piano music anybody* ever *composed, and (I believe) the most popular ring tone on mobile phones in this 21st century.*

Thus, like Giulietta Guicciardi, Therese Malfatti also achieves immortality thanks to her acquaintanceship with Beethoven.

Time and again the mystery has been declared solved. Yet still it rages.

As with so much about Beethoven, let's start with what we *do* know. On the morning of 6 July, in the Bohemian spa town of Teplitz (today Bad Teplice in the Czech Republic) Beethoven sat down in a hotel room and began writing a letter. In the evening he added to it. The next morning he added yet more, before finishing it.

The letter runs to nearly 10 pages, and is a deeply passionate love letter. It begins:

Mein Engel, mein Alles, mein Ich [My Angel, My All, My Very Self]

It begins in a matter-of-fact way, describing his difficult coach journey from Prague, but is followed by passages of sheer erotic intensity – not something he ever did in any other writing or is reported by anyone as having ever said. You think I exaggerate? Try this:

My soul is so full of things to tell you – Oh – There are times when words are simply no use – remain my only true darling, my all, as I am yours . . . If only we could live together, what a life it is!!!! Now!!!! Without you . . . As much as you love me – I love you even more deeply . . . Oh, God – so near! So far! is our love not sent from Heaven? And is it not even as firm as the firmament of Heaven?

And then, in the final passage, those three words that have entered Beethoven legend: *Meine unsterbliche Geliebte [My Immortal Beloved]:*

Even lying in bed thoughts of you force themselves into my head, my Immortal Beloved . . . I can only live with you wholly or not at all, yes, I have even decided to wander helplessly, until I can fly into your arms, and say that I have found my haven there, my soul embraced by you to be transported to the kingdom of spirits . . . Never can another woman possess my heart – never, never . . . Love me today – yesterday – what tearful longing for you – you – you – my life – my all – Farewell – Love me still – never misjudge the most faithful heart of your beloved . . . L. ever mine, ever thine, ever ours.

Convinced? Now begin the speculation and the theories. Nowhere in the letter does he name the woman or give us any clue as to her identity. Nor does he say where she is. Nor does he date the letter by year. But there is a lot we can fill in.

We know, for a start, that he registered his arrival in Teplitz with the police (as travellers were required to do), and so we can date the year as 1812. He also refers to the place where the woman is staying as K. It is beyond doubt that that was the Bohemian spa town of Karlsbad (today Karlovy Vary in the Czech Republic). We can also deduce from the letter that the woman had been in Prague in the preceding days, where their love affair had taken place.

Given the requirement to register with the police, given the date and locations, it is reasonable to conclude that in order to identify the mystery woman, we must be able to ascertain that she was in Prague in the first week of July 1812 and then in Karlsbad following that.

As for the letter itself, it was found in Beethoven's effects in the days following his death, nearly 15 years after it was written. What does that tell us? Either that he never sent it (he says in the letter he missed the post). Or that he sent it and the woman gave it back to him.

Given that there are no postmarks on it, the most likely explanation is that he never sent it. It's more than likely that later, having got over it, his passions having cooled, he decided to hide it away. It must have been a deliberate decision on his part not to mention her name in the letter – difficult to write a letter like that without using her name even once. That, and using just the letter K to identify where she was, is pretty convincing evidence that he wanted none of this to come out. The fact that he kept the letter for the rest of his life in a secret drawer, and that it stayed there every time he moved residence, is the clincher: he wanted no one to know about the love affair.

Conspiracy theorists will point out that there is yet another possible explanation. Beethoven wrote the whole thing as a hoax. He was not averse to a practical joke (he played one once on a fellow musician), and he enjoyed making (pretty poor) puns in his letters.

But this letter is clearly written in the white heat of passion. Also the tone of it is actually quite negative: he is seeking to persuade the woman that their love affair cannot endure – the odds are stacked too heavily against them. That does not have the makings of a practical joke. And if that was what it was, would he have bothered going into details about the journey, even about the problems he had with his hotel booking, and the fact that he misread the postal times and missed the next available mail coach?

No, Beethoven was not that kind of man. We can therefore state categorically that in the first week of July 1812 Beethoven had a brief and passionate love affair with a woman in Prague. In the days following he wrote this letter to her, trying to make her understand that theirs was an impossible love. He never sent the letter, choosing instead to hide it away, and keeping it in his possession for the rest of his life.

All this is important enough to anyone with the slightest interest in Beethoven's life. What elevates it even beyond that is that it is completely clear from the letter that the woman was in love with him. It is, as far as we know, the only time in his life that he had a full-blown affair with a woman who clearly returned his love.

So who was she?

The Likely Lasses

From a large field, it is generally agreed that the two main contenders are Antonie Brentano and Josephine Deym.

Of these two only Antonie fits the criteria. She *was* in Prague in the first week of July 1812, and she *was* in Karlsbad following that. In fact, of all the women whose names have ever been put forward as the Immortal Beloved, Antonie is the only one who we know for certain was in both the right places at the right times.

Beethoven knew Antonie well in Vienna; indeed for a period when Antonie was unwell, he would go to her house, sit at the piano in the anteroom outside her bedroom, and play soothing music for her day after day.

The possibility for mutual attraction was certainly there. They would without doubt have spent intimate moments together at her house, and meeting up in Prague – away from Vienna, away from home, away from friends – might have allowed their passion to erupt.

There was one enormous obstacle, though. I said "away from home, away from friends", but *not* away from family. Antonie was married, with children, and her husband and one of her children were with her in both Prague and Karlsbad. All three were in poor health and had gone to Bohemia to take the waters (as had Beethoven).

The fact that Antonie was married actually allows us to make more sense of the letter. No wonder Beethoven talks of an obstacle that cannot be overcome. No wonder he points out that he and his lover can never be wholly together. Indeed, in his words you can sense the moral struggle he is undergoing with the realization that he is in love with a married woman.

Josephine is an entirely different kettle of fish. Whereas Antonie comes across as a level-headed married woman and mother whose husband was a successful merchant, Josephine endured two dreadful marriages and was (no doubt as a result) nervous, overwrought and highly strung. Beethoven had come to know her when he took her (and her sister) on as pupils, and it was well known that he was highly attracted to her.

He stood no chance of pursuing his suit, though, for Josephine – born into the aristocratic Hungarian family of Brunsvik – was more or less forced into marriage by her mother, who saw that a certain Count Joseph Deym had eyes only for Josephine, was a wealthy and highly respected art dealer, and moved in the highest social circles. The fact that he was 30 years Josephine's senior was no hindrance. Mother and daughter only learned after Josephine had married him that Deym was a scoundrel, was heavily in debt, and was even forced to leave Vienna for a time to avoid his creditors. He did Josephine the favour of dying early, but not before fathering four children on her.

Six years later she married an awful man who would almost certainly qualify today as a wife-beater. She had three more children, and when her husband decided to leave her, he forcibly wrenched his children from her arms and took them with him.

But wait – what happened in that six-year period when she was between husbands? Remarkably, as recently as 1949 (yes, 1949) 13 letters from Beethoven to Josephine, written in that period, were discovered, in which he pleads with her for a physical relationship. She left it to her sister to reply on her behalf, turning him down.

But could the second bad marriage have caused her to reconsider? And could she have travelled to Prague in early July 1812 where she met Beethoven, before going on to Karlsbad?

If she did, then she must have made the whole journey incognito. Europe was at war. No one could cross borders without passports and without registering with the local police. Josephine would have had to manage all this without arousing any suspicion at all – not of the authorities, nor of her family and friends back in Vienna, who make no mention of her absence.

In the end you are forced to say that we can prove Antonie fits the criteria to be the Immortal Beloved.

In Josephine's case we can only say that there is nothing to prove she cannot be.

Now here's a funny thing. I have discussed all this with a number of males and females. I have put this question to each one: *Antonie was a respectable married woman with children, staying with her husband and child in a hotel in Prague. Could she possibly have given them the slip to have a brief passionate affair with Beethoven, apparently arousing no suspicion in her husband?*

Without exception the males have said no, and the females – with a knowing smile – have said yes.

Appetite for more conspiracy? Both Antonie and Josephine gave birth roughly nine months after Prague. Antonie's son Karl – her first child for seven years – was born physically and mentally impaired, and died at the age of 37. Josephine's daughter Minona was to live into her 80s and died a spinster. All her life it was rumoured she was Beethoven's daughter. Is her name a clue? Minona – *Anonim* backwards. The child with no name. I have seen a picture of her. She was the image of Beethoven, which proves nothing.

There is one other possible candidate for the Immortal Beloved, and she may be the most likely. A woman as yet unknown to history. If Beethoven's letters to Josephine only surfaced in 1949, who

knows what might be lurking in someone's attic
somewhere in the world . . . ?

Attic and Shoebox

. . . On that very note, soon after I had taken part
in a BBC documentary about the life of Beethoven,
and had published the first book in my trilogy on
his life, *The Last Master*, I received a letter from a
young woman living near Paris. In her mother's
attic, she said, was a shoebox containing
correspondence between Minona and her aunt.
There were also effects belonging to Beethoven, and
a hitherto unknown and unpublished letter of
Beethoven to Josephine. The handwriting had been
authenticated, she told me. The letters contained
sensational information, she wrote, and she wanted
to talk to me about them.

We spoke on the phone, and she told me that
Beethoven's letter proved Minona was his daughter
by Josephine, and that Josephine was therefore
beyond doubt the Immortal Beloved. She further
said that she and her mother were directly
descended from Minona, and were therefore directly
descended from Beethoven himself. It was clear
from the way she spoke that she knew very intimate
and intricate details of Josephine's life.

The young woman told me she was prepared to
meet me and we set up a meeting at a London

hotel in the following week. Sensing that a third party, calm and rational, might be a good idea, I asked if my wife could accompany me. She agreed.

The next evening I received a call from a well-spoken man who described himself as the woman's uncle. He told me sternly that wanting to introduce a third party to the meeting was unacceptable. I pointed out that it was purely so there would be someone to help me take notes, and help me form an opinion on what I had heard. He said the family were very worried about adverse publicity. We were dealing here with secrets that had been in the family for generations, and they greatly feared media publicity. He said he would phone again the next morning.

He did. It was a curt conversation. His niece was unwell. She could not attend the meeting. Better not to proceed anyway, he said. I asked him if he could understand why it was just possible I might consider the whole episode a hoax. "You must be guided by your instincts," he said. I never heard from them again. I have no address. The mobile phone number I had been given was soon discontinued.

The mystery lingers . . .

Ludwig "von" Beethoven, "Nobleman"

There's no escaping it, no turning a blind eye, no moving swiftly on, no pretending none of it ever happened. If only we could wave it away, dismiss it casually, one of those things, not important. It cannot be done. We have to be bold. We must confront it.

For a period of nearly five years, Ludwig van Beethoven – supreme artist, greatest living composer, revered and respected across Europe – behaved in an unforgivably reprehensible way, was cruel and vindictive, selfish and jealous.

His few friends then were appalled, and we today must struggle to accept that the creator of such sublime music could behave in this way. But who said artists should always be nice people? And if we are to afford Beethoven any sympathy at all, it can only be on the basis that two centuries ago his behaviour may have shocked, but in the context of the time it was acceptable. Not only that, but in the end he won.

Yes, he won. But at what a cost – to his already fragile health, and to his artistic creativity. The victor emerged with his health broken, and for a substantial period he was unable to produce any composition of significance.

It is not an exaggeration to say that this trauma, entirely self-inflicted, sitting like a massive dead weight in Beethoven's life, hastened his death. Yet at the same time – contradiction after contradiction, as always with Beethoven – in the few years left to him, as his health deteriorated, his deafness became total, he withdrew ever deeper into his own thoughts, sought less and less from those around him . . . so his work became more profound, and he produced the greatest compositions of all.

"I Appoint My Brother, Ludwig . . ."

The nightmare began on 15 November 1815, the day that Beethoven's brother Caspar Carl died at the

age of 41 of consumption. You'll remember that Beethoven had no liking for Carl's wife, Johanna, believing her to be a deeply immoral woman.

It appears he had finally managed to convince his brother of this, because nearly three years earlier, when he first fell seriously ill, Carl had drawn up a written statement of a single paragraph, stating that after his death it was his wish that his brother Ludwig should undertake the guardianship of his son Karl. He signed in the presence of three witnesses.

Carl's health recovered, and the document was not enacted. But by late 1815 the consumption had taken hold, there was a sudden deterioration, and it was clear Carl was close to death.

On a single day a remarkable sequence of events occurred. We only have Beethoven's word for what happened, but taking his account and adding a few elements he will no doubt have suppressed, we can construct the likely scenario.

On Tuesday 14 November Carl van Beethoven, on his deathbed and with his lawyer and three (new) witnesses present, as well as his wife Johanna, drew up his will. It contained just eight paragraphs. Paragraph 5 read:

Along with my wife I appoint my brother Ludwig van Beethoven co-guardian [of my son Karl].

Carl signed his will probably around 2 or 3 o'clock in the afternoon. An hour or so later Ludwig arrived to see his brother, who by now was alone. He saw the will, picked it up and read it. Paragraph 5 hit him like a thunderbolt. He shouted at Carl: "*What are you thinking of? You can't mean it! You can't leave it like this. It goes against everything we agreed.*"

It must have been an extraordinary scene. Carl was little more than 12 hours from death. One imagines him propped up in bed, his small frame ravaged by disease, his cheeks flushed in the characteristic sign of tuberculosis, probably racked by coughing, a handkerchief held to his lips, gazing in despair with feverish watery eyes . . . as his brother strides across the end of the bed, waving the will and ranting against Johanna.

It's quite possible that at this moment Beethoven even gave vent to a rumour which was circulating: Johanna was pregnant, and everyone knew it could not be by her husband. (It might have been true, though Johanna did not subsequently give birth. More likely she was having an affair, and word had got out.)

Whatever he said, it was enough to convince the dying man, who had lost all power of resistance. Carl took the pen Beethoven handed him and crossed out the words:

Along with my wife and *co-*

Beethoven, satisfied with his efforts, left his brother, but returned to see him around an hour and a half or two hours later. The will had gone: "*Where is it? What's happened? Who's taken it? Tell me! Tell me!*"

Carl, with failing strength and struggling to speak, knowing the torrent he was about to unleash, told his brother that people had come to see him, something had been added to the will and he had been made to sign it: "*Who were they? What did they want? What did they add? It's to do with Karl, isn't it? You must tell me!*"

Beethoven rushed out of the room and raced to the lawyer's office. It was by now late afternoon and the office was closed. Beethoven realized there was nothing more he could do until the next day.

The following morning at 5 o'clock, in the chill pre-dawn darkness of a November morning, Carl died.

God Permit Them To Be Harmonious

At the reading of the will, Beethoven's worst fears were realized. There was a codicil at the end of the will, which had not been there before and about which he had therefore known nothing. The lawyer read it:

I have found it necessary to add to my will that I by no means desire that my son be taken from his mother, but that he shall always . . . remain with his mother, to which end his guardianship is to be exercised by her as well as my brother.

Beethoven literally could not believe his ears. His mind must have raced as he struggled to understand what had happened. It was simple. In Beethoven's short absence from his brother's room, Johanna had come in, seen the will and discovered to her horror that the crucial words granting her co-guardianship of her son had been crossed out.

She hastily summoned her lawyer, who came with the same three witnesses. He drafted the codicil, Carl signed it, followed by the witnesses.

The final sentence of the codicil read:

God permit them to be harmonious for the sake of my child's welfare. This is the last wish of the dying husband and brother.

Carl cannot, in his worst fears, have imagined just how far his last wish would come from being realized.

Beethoven had been duped, fooled, bested, wronged. His blood was up. He went on the attack.

Most Worshipful Imperial . . .

What would you do if you were a friend of
Beethoven? I know what I'd do. Sit him down,
reason with him, point out Johanna was after all the
boy's mother, encourage him to talk to her; failing
that, offer to talk to her on his behalf, and so on. It
is beyond doubt that his friends did just that,
because in the period immediately following, there
is virtually no mention of any of them. It is as if
they have vanished. Why? Obviously, having tried
to reason and failed, they stepped well back, out of
the line of fire.

Let us also give the lawyers the benefit of the doubt,
and assume they tried to reason with him too. If
they did, they too failed. If they did not, well, it is
not exactly unheard of to find a lawyer who
practises the reverse of the lawyer's motto,
"negotiate, don't litigate", salivating at the prospect
of the fat fees to come.

No, there was no reasoning with him. He decided
to challenge the legality of the will in court, and in
so doing made arguably the single worst decision of
his life.

Under his lawyer's instruction and in his lawyer's
hand, he submitted an application on 28 November
1815 to the *Imperial and Royal Landrecht of Lower
Austria*, the upper court strictly for members of the

nobility, urging their Most Worshipful Imperial Lordships to recognize his sole claim to the guardianship of Karl. At the same time he asked the magistrate's office to supply him with a copy of Johanna's conviction for embezzlement (the affair of the pearl necklace). This was refused, but he was informed the necessary documentation would be forwarded to the *Landrecht*.

Note that he applied to the *Landrecht*, court of the nobility, not to the *Magistrat*, the commoners' court. Neither he, nor his lawyer, nor anyone else, thought this at all unusual.

So far, so good, and there was no real surprise, given Beethoven's musical fame and reputation, Johanna's notoriety and criminal record, and the attitudes of the day, that on 9 January 1816 – after Beethoven had appeared before the court to give testimony, pointing out the codicil was added without his knowledge and behind his back, and his dying brother had only agreed because he did not have the strength to resist – he was granted his wish. He was declared sole guardian of Karl.

End of story. Not. How he must have wished.

Very soon Beethoven discovered what it was like to be a single parent. Karl was 9 years of age. He had seen his father die, his mother's name publicly blackened by his uncle, and had now been taken

away from his mother. This does not make for an easy child.

Beethoven's first act was to put Karl into a boarding school – in Vienna, true, but a boarding school nevertheless. Later in the year Karl complained of severe stomach pains and had to undergo a hernia operation, after which he needed to wear a truss. Beethoven had no idea how to handle the situation.

With Karl at least under his control, it was now time to begin the process of turning him into a musician, the Beethoven of the next generation. He instructed his pupil Carl Czerny (yes, he of the hundreds of piano exercises) to teach the boy. Czerny reported back that the boy had no musical talent whatsoever. *Then teach him harder!*

Beethoven did not have the slightest notion of how to look after a normal boy of 9, let alone one who had just had an operation and who today we might well describe as having learning difficulties, who alternated between hyperactivity and sullenness, who showed no respect for his uncle and clearly pined for his mother.

Immediately after the hernia operation, he summoned Karl down to Baden and took him hill walking, losing patience when the boy complained of pain from the wound. There is anecdotal evidence of furious rows. Karl, lying in bed, lashed out in frustration at his uncle: Beethoven was seen with a scar on his face.

Johanna was as desperate to see her son as he was to see her. She apparently tried to visit the school in Vienna secretly, disguising herself as a servant, and even on one occasion as a man. But Beethoven had befriended the head teacher (or more likely threatened and intimidated him), and the luckless man reported Johanna's ill-fated attempts to see her son.

Beethoven soon lost confidence in the head teacher and removed Karl from the school. Instead he moved Karl into his own apartment and hired a private tutor. Pre-teenage boy lives with eccentric middle-aged composer now so deaf he has to get people to write down what they say to him, whose clothes are always untidy and in need of repair, who is the object of stares and taunts from urchins when he goes out, who finds restaurants reserve a table for him alone so other patrons are protected from his unsavoury manners. Not a recipe for success. A friend recalls Beethoven saying in anguish:

Karl is ashamed of me!

Beethoven decided to spend the summer of 1818 in the picturesque village of Mödling, south of Vienna on the road down to Baden. He entered Karl in the local school. After a month Karl was expelled for bad behaviour.

In the midst of all this turmoil, Beethoven composed arguably his greatest piano sonata (certainly the longest and most complex), the *Hammerklavier Opus 106* – composing virtually nothing of significance in the year before or after. (Beethoven, man of contradictions.)

On the basis that Beethoven was impeding her son's proper education, Johanna twice petitioned the *Landrecht* to reconsider its decision to exclude her from Karl's guardianship. Both times her appeals were rejected.

On 3 December 1818, Karl took matters into his own hands and ran away . . . to his mother. Beethoven summoned the police. They demanded that Johanna hand over her son to Beethoven in compliance with the court order.

But Johanna used the fact that Karl had run away from Beethoven to her to petition the court yet again. All three principal players – Beethoven, Johanna, and Karl – were called to give evidence. Separately.

And this is where Beethoven's world fell in.

Herr von Beethoven

Karl, now just turned 12, gave nervous and anxious answers favouring his uncle over his mother, which he knew he had to do since the original court order had gone against his mother. He spoke highly of his uncle, with one exception:

Q. Has your uncle ever maltreated you?
A. Only once, after I ran away to my mother, and the police made me go back to my uncle.
Q. What did your uncle do?
A. He threatened to throttle me.

What a dreadfully intimidating and unnatural thing for a 12 year old to have to do – go into the witness box in court and testify in front of a panel of judges.

Johanna's testimony, as quoted in the court minutes, was calm and assured. Why else would her son come to her, if not because he did not like living with his uncle? She had indeed advised him to return, but Karl was reluctant to do so in case his uncle punished him. A relative of hers confirmed to the court that when Karl ran away to his mother, he was dirty, inadequately dressed for winter, and had chilblains on his hands and feet.

Johanna also told the court she believed Beethoven intended sending Karl away to a private school outside Vienna. She wanted him to go to the local public school, where he would mix with other boys and be in the familiar surroundings of the city. Furthermore, she had been assured there was a place available for him there.

Beethoven entered the witness box, his lawyer no doubt whispering the judges' questions straight into his ear because of his deafness:

Q. Why are you not in agreement for the boy to attend the Imperial and Royal University seminary here in Vienna?
A. There are too many pupils there and discipline is too lax.
Q. Where then do you propose sending him?
A. I would return him to the boarding school for the winter, then to the private seminary in Melk [several hours' carriage ride along the Danube west of Vienna]. *Or, if only he were of noble birth, to the Theresianum academy* [in Vienna].

That last sentence, thrown in almost as an aside, was what sank him. The panel of judges must have sat aghast at his words, then exchanged looks of incredulity:

Q. But does your family not belong to the nobility? Are you not of noble birth, Herr von Beethoven? Does not the von *prefix to your name signify that you are of noble birth? If not, would you explain to the court why you originally brought this case before the Imperial and Royal Landrecht, and not the court of the common people?*

Beethoven was ordered to produce documents proving his noble birth, which of course he was unable to do. The *Landrecht* handed the case down to the lower court, the *Magistrat*, who found against Beethoven and in favour of Johanna.

Beethoven's humiliation was complete. It was the topic of conversation on everyone's lips, in every café, restaurant, and on every street corner. The famous composer, so upright, moralistic and noble, so contemptuous of lesser morals in others, was after all a mere commoner of Flemish descent. All those people whom he had never bothered to correct when they addressed him as *Herr* von *Beethoven* now knew the humiliating truth. And to cap it all, he'd lost the case he should never have brought in the first place!

My Last Attempt

But Beethoven was not finished. After several fruitless attempts to persuade the Magistrat to change its mind, in February 1820, with the help of a new lawyer, he drew up a huge document – the longest piece of writing that exists in Beethoven's hand – and submitted it to the Court of Appeal, the highest court in the land:

This is my last attempt to save my nephew, and for his sake I am prepared to submit myself to this humiliation.

It is long and rambling, petty and vindictive. It goes into every aspect of Johanna's behaviour, portraying

her as wicked and immoral, with no education whatsoever, and utterly unsuited to bringing up her son. Beethoven even blames her for Karl's hernia!

And do you know what? He won. Yes, he won. What on earth brought about this extraordinary turn around? We will never know. One of his friends had told him that the *Magistrat* was known to be corrupt, and if he had used bribery he would undoubtedly have won at that earlier stage. Might he have used bribery with the Court of Appeal? There is no evidence he did, but there wouldn't be, would there?

Johanna made a last desperate appeal to the emperor himself to intervene. His Imperial Royal Highness refused. The case was finally over. Karl was at last Beethoven's, to bring up as he saw fit – the boy's mother excluded.

Not long afterwards Beethoven fell ill. He recovered. But rheumatic fever followed, and then jaundice. In fact, for most of the next year he was very ill indeed.

Beethoven had little more than six years to live. It really is not an exaggeration to say his health was irretrievably broken, and that he never fully recovered.

Yet still to come were the *Missa Solemnis*, the *Choral Symphony*, the *Diabelli Variations*, the *Piano*

Sonatas Opp. 109, 110, 111, all five of the great late *String Quartets Opp. 127, 130, 131, 132, 135.*

Collectively, then, the greatest music Beethoven – or, let's be frank, any other composer – had ever written.

Which is far from saying all was well. Karl was to exact his revenge for what his uncle had put him through, in the most terrible way imaginable. What Beethoven had sown, he was to reap.

A New Flower Glows

The greatest symphony ever written nearly did not get performed at all. Beethoven is now a 53-year-old man in appalling health. Three years earlier, the court case barely over, in a dreadful few months he developed rheumatic fever, followed by jaundice. Barely recovered from that, he suffered chest pains. He has constant ear ache – *my usual trouble* – and, of course, is profoundly deaf.

He has few close friends. With the exception of Stephan von Breuning, whom he has known since childhood, most of them are musicians, who accord him respect rather than friendship. His relationship with his nephew – his "son" – Karl has gone from bad to worse.

Amidst all this he has brought to fruition a project he has carried in his mind for more than 30 years. Beethoven had known, and admired, Schiller's poetry since his student days. He first talked of setting Schiller's *An die Freude [Ode to Joy]* in 1793. Eighteen years later he scribbled down a very basic setting of the first line to music. Six years after that he began work on a new symphony, set it aside, and did not begin serious work for another five years. We have reached 1822. By February 1824 he has completed his crowning work.

Few friends he may have had, but Ludwig van Beethoven was the most famous artist in Vienna, in Austria, in Europe. He was lionized wherever he went; his music was heard in salons and concert halls across Europe. Word had spread in Vienna that he was working on a new symphony, and that it was going to be revolutionary. *Voices? In a symphony? Never been done before.* Managers, publishers, musicians, patrons . . . all held their breath, waiting for the moment.

Who, then, can we blame for the fact that this new work nearly did not get performed at all? Why, none other than Herr Beethoven himself, of course.

When he could have had his pick of the theatres in Vienna, what did Beethoven do? He wrote to the General Manager of the Berlin Theatre, inquiring whether his new symphony, along with the newly completed *Missa Solemnis*, might receive its first performance there. In Berlin, capital of Prussia. Prussia, enemy of Austria. The manager, a certain Count Brühl, wrote back saying he was honoured and delighted and would arrange it.

What was Beethoven thinking of? In poor health, deaf, was he really contemplating travelling hundreds of miles to a strange city, organizing and rehearsing an orchestra unfamiliar with his work, risking a frosty reception from an audience unused to his eccentricities, both personal and musical?

I doubt it. If, on the other hand, he wanted to jolt the musical establishment of Vienna, he was successful beyond his dreams. No fewer than 30 of its leading lights signed a lengthy letter to him, which they made public:

Withhold no longer . . . a performance of the latest masterworks of your hands . . . We know that a new flower glows in the garland of your glorious, still unequalled Symphonies . . . For years we have waited and hoped to see you distribute new gifts from the fullness of your riches to the circle of your friends . . . Do not any longer disappoint everybody's expectations! . . . Do not allow these, your latest offspring, some day

*to appear as foreigners in their place of birth,
introduced by persons to whom you and your mind are
strange! Appear soon among your friends, your
admirers, your venerators!*

Hardly surprisingly, it did the trick. *It is very
beautiful! It rejoices me greatly!*

Problem solved. Plans to perform the *Ninth
Symphony* and *Missa Solemnis* went ahead. But I said
the *Ninth* nearly did not get performed *at all*, not
that it nearly did not get performed *in Vienna*.

Yes, and once again it was the Master himself, and
he alone, who was to blame.

The obvious choice of venue was the Theater an der
Wien, the privately owned theatre outside the city
wall where so many of Beethoven's works had first
been heard. But Beethoven objected to the theatre's
resident conductor, as well as its orchestra leader.
The theatre manager, Count Palffy, agreed to
replace the conductor. The leader was more of a
problem – replace him, and he might take some of
the orchestra with him.

In compensation Palffy offered to provide theatre,
staff, musicians, for a knockdown price of 1200
florins. But there was a problem. Beethoven could
not stand Palffy. It dated back many years to when
Beethoven was performing in a salon. Palffy was in

the small audience, carrying on a loud conversation with a lady. Several times Beethoven called on him to be quiet, without success. Finally he broke off playing and shouted:

I will not play for such pigs!

No surprise, then, when Beethoven rejected Palffy's offer and began negotiations with another theatre, the Kärntnertor. Palffy, desperate, dropped his price even lower. It did the trick. Beethoven agreed.

But the orchestra leader refused to yield his place.

> *Ironically, the orchestra leader was none other than Franz Clement, formerly a great friend of Beethoven, for whom he had composed the Violin Concerto and who had given it its first performance. It is not known why Beethoven subsequently went off Clement to such a degree, other than the fact that Clement became increasingly known for using a showy technique in performance to hide a decline in his skills.*

Worse, the entire orchestra fell in behind him. *He goes and we all go.*

Meanwhile, unknown to his patrons, or either of the theatre managers involved, Beethoven had instructed his brother and nephew to open negotiations with a *third* theatre.

When his patrons discovered this, they came up with the rather foolish idea of a practical joke (you'll try anything if it works) involving making Beethoven sign a document committing himself to a decision. He saw through it, and that was it:

I despise treachery. Do not visit me any more. There will be no concert.

Do you see how close the *Ninth* came to never being performed at all? Well, I haven't finished yet . . .

Beethoven relented, of course, and settled on the Kärntnertor. Palffy dropped his price to *zero*! No good. He should never have chatted up that lady while Beethoven was playing.

So the venue, and date, were fixed. Now the problem was selecting the soloists. The first choice for soprano was swiftly rejected, and the popular Henriette Sontag employed in her place. There was no doubt over the contralto: it was to be the Hungarian Karoline Unger. The preferred tenor refused to sing, claiming the part was too low for his voice. The chosen bass claimed his part was too high.

Four singers, a chorus and orchestra were finally assembled. There was only time for two rehearsals. The second, and final one, was a disaster. The singers were all over the place, demanding that

Beethoven simplify their parts. The chorus master
pointed out that his sopranos could not sustain the
fortissimo high A for the 14 bars that he demanded –
*Did it not occur to you Herr Beethoven that they need
to breathe?* – (Sopranos still complain about it
today!)

Karoline Unger threw a tantrum in front of
everyone. "You are a tyrant over all the vocal
organs!" she yelled at Beethoven. At the very last
minute the bass soloist pulled out, and was replaced
by a chorus member.

Beethoven, on the day of the concert, washed his
hands of the whole thing. Then changed his mind
yet again. *That* is how near the glorious *Ninth* came
to never being performed at all.

> *For the performance Beethoven was required to wear a black
> tailcoat, but did not own one. Instead he wore a green coat,
> and under it a white cravat and waistcoat, black satin
> breeches, black silk stockings, and shoes with buckles.*

It should have been a disaster, of course. It was a
triumph. Beethoven had insisted on standing on
stage alongside the conductor to help him with the
beat (!). At the end of the symphony there occurred
one of those moments that has become legend, one
of the most moving in the life of this supreme and
supremely difficult composer, one even the
contemplation of which can move me to tears.

The final *fortissimo* chord sounded and the audience erupted, applauding wildly, waving hats and handkerchiefs in the air, calling Beethoven's name.

He himself, deaf, oblivious to all around him, hearing the sounds of his work only in his head, continued to wave his arms, conducting his own imaginary orchestra. Karoline Unger, the contralto – the one who had thrown the tantrum – stepped forward and tugged on his sleeve.

He looked up at her, his face frozen in alarm. "*What? What is it? Has it . . . ? Am I . . . ?*"

Smiling, she gestured towards the audience and gently turned him round.

He saw hundreds of cheering faces, mouths open, hands clapping, hats and handkerchiefs in the air, lips silently mouthing his name, the noise and vibration registering in his head like a thousand tiny explosions.

Beethoven had given the world his greatest work.

A Turbulent End

That Poisonous Breath

Theatre managers, orchestral players, singers, prima donnas, divas . . . small wonder Beethoven turned to the most intimate, most intense of all musical forms, the string quartet. Between now, 1824, and the end of his life less than three years away, he produced no fewer than five quartets, collectively known as the *Late Quartets*, his greatest quartets, arguably his greatest single body of work.

He is now profoundly deaf. He hears certain distorted sounds and feels vibration. But the beauty

of music, its harmonies, are lost to him. Yet he composes his most profound work.

> It has been argued that he could not have composed the Late Quartets without being deaf. Their sheer profundity reflects something beyond the normal human condition. If that is true, it is sobering to reflect that had Beethoven lived today, and if modern medicine and microscopic surgery had been able to cure his deafness, we might never have had the Late Quartets. The single greatest tragedy of Beethoven's life, his deafness, undoubtedly contributed to his greatest gifts to mankind.

Just as with the *Ninth Symphony*, his achievement is all the greater, given that while composing, creating, his life was so comprehensively going off the rails. It is as if Beethoven *needed* tension, stress and pressure to enable him to write. This is a man in such emotional turmoil that on one occasion, wandering aimlessly in a suburb staring into windows, he is arrested as a tramp by a policeman who refuses to believe he is Beethoven, and spends the night in police jail.

It is, of course, his relationship with Karl which dominates his final years. Think of how it could have been. *World famous composer, basking in the glory of his* Ninth Symphony, *aware his health is declining, makes peace with his sister-in-law, admits he has been harsh over the years with his nephew, refuses to allow his deafness to stop him socializing with fellow musicians, enjoys a glass of wine or more with friends . . .*

Stop, stop! This is Ludwig van Beethoven we are dealing with here, a man whose lifelong motto might have been *Why make it easy when you can make it difficult?*

In the months following the famous premiere of the *Ninth*, Karl was a student at the University of Vienna studying philology. He was now approaching his 18th birthday. Beethoven had clearly abandoned any hope that his nephew might one day become a musician, but he was clearly totally unprepared for the bombshell of a decision Karl had in store for him. It's all there, recorded in a conversation book because of Beethoven's deafness. We have half the conversation – Karl's half, naturally – but it does not take too much imagination for us to fill in Beethoven's responses:

Karl	*You will find my choice rather strange, but please let me speak freely. The profession I would like to follow is not a* common *one. It still demands study, only of a different kind, and it is of a sort that I enjoy.*
Beethoven	*Well, come on. Out with it! What is it?*
Karl	*Soldier*
Beethoven	*What?! Soldier?! You want to be a soldier?! Have you totally taken leave of*

> *your senses? A Beethoven becoming a*
> *soldier? We are artists! Who put you up*
> *to this ridiculous idea?*

Karl   *Nobody at all.*

Beethoven resolutely forbade it, and he got his
way – for the moment. But there was more trouble
in store for Karl. That autumn Beethoven was
staying down in Baden, and word reached him that
Karl was keeping bad company, staying out late at
night, sometimes not returning to his bed at all:
18 year old boy, young man, drinks to celebrate
coming of age, parties with fellow students . . . What
parent would be surprised to learn that? Is there any
other way for an 18-year-old student to behave?

Karl made the mistake of bringing his best friend, a
fellow student named Joseph Niemetz, to meet
Beethoven in Baden. Beethoven formed an instant
dislike of the young man. Later – again, it is all
written down – Beethoven forbade Karl to continue
seeing Niemetz, who is "rough and common". He
even expresses a fear in very roundabout language
that Niemetz is taking Karl to prostitutes, which
will inevitably lead to venereal disease – "that
poisonous breath coming from dragons".

If you're wondering how much more Karl can take,
you're right. But it was to be another year, during
which Beethoven berated him one moment, loved
him the next, fired off an angry letter one moment,

pleaded for forgiveness the next, before he exacted his terrible revenge.

And all through this fraught period of tension, arguments, poor health, Beethoven continued to compose his *Late Quartets*.

Ever more worried about his wayward (normal) nephew, Beethoven imposed more and more restrictions upon him. He ordered colleagues to follow the young man and report back on his activities. One tempted Karl to a game of billiards, established that he was not very good, and was able to reassure Beethoven that his nephew had obviously not spent too much time playing the game. Worried that Karl was gambling, his uncle made him account for every penny he spent.

And then . . . the ultimate, the worst. Oh, the horror of it, the sinful, dreadful, appalling, unbearable horror of it. When word reached Beethoven, he simply could not believe it. Karl had done . . . *what*? No, not prostitutes, not gambling, drinking, or billiards. Far, far worse. Karl had been in secret to see *his mother*.

Beethoven was completely beside himself. There was a showdown with Karl. There was a fight. They came to blows.

Karl, finally, had had enough.

The Rauhenstein Ruins

In the first week of August 1826 Karl pawned his watch and with the money bought two pistols and gunpowder. He took the carriage south to Baden. There he chose his uncle's favourite hill walk – out on the main road west of the town, to the thickly wooded Helenenthal, the valley with tree-covered hills. He chose the hill on the top of which stood the ruins of the medieval Rauhenstein abbey, its damaged towers sticking like sharp and broken fingers into the sky.

He climbed one of the towers, loaded the first pistol, put it to his head, and fired. The bullet missed. He loaded the second pistol, put it to his head, and fired. The bullet tore along his temple, searing the thin flesh, before flying harmlessly off.

Karl staggered down from the tower and collapsed. Some time later he was found by hill walkers, who took him to his . . . *mother*.

Beethoven's world fell in. Not only had his nephew, his *son*, tried to kill himself, he had then been taken to his *mother*. Everything, everything Beethoven had fought for, struggled to achieve, gone through the courts to win, had come to nothing.

To make matters worse, Vienna was awash with the story. Just as his humiliation in court nearly eight years before had been the talk of every coffee house and restaurant in the city, once again he was the sole topic of conversation. *Have you heard? Have you heard? The great man's nephew tried to kill himself! Then he was taken to his mother! Hah! How will the deaf old fool handle this? If you want my opinion, it'll finish him off . . .*

Karl was moved from his mother's to Vienna General Hospital where, as an attempted suicide, he was made by law to receive religious instruction. The police report stated:

Karl's paternal guardian [Beethoven] has proved little able to give him adequate moral principles.

Insult to injury. Beethoven's distress soon turned to anger. He went to the hospital, stopped a doctor in the corridor, and demanded:

Is my scoundrel of a nephew in your ward?

When Beethoven identified himself, the doctor (who related the incident many years later) could not believe the shabbily dressed, unkempt individual talking to him was the great Beethoven. (Just as the policeman who had arrested him had been unable to. And there are more instances like this to come.)

With perfect timing Beethoven's younger brother Johann wrote to him, inviting him to get away from

Vienna, escape from the wagging tongues, bring Karl and come and stay with him and his wife in his country estate in Gneixendorf, nearly two days' carriage ride west of Vienna along the Danube.

It should have been an ideal break. It was a disaster.

Who is this madman?

Beethoven was already ill when he and Karl left Vienna for Gneixendorf in late September. His stomach, ankles and lower legs were swollen. The disease which would kill him within six months – cirrhosis of the liver – was taking hold.

Once again, it could have been so normal. *Beethoven stays with brother and sister-in-law in idyllic countryside, lovingly nursing his nephew back to health* . . . Once again, this is Beethoven.

For a start, he loathed his brother and detested his sister-in-law. Sounds strong language, but it is true. He considered his younger brother Johann a total fool, incapable of a rational decision, who had stumbled through life making one mistake after another.

Soon after Johann had bought his country estate, he wrote a letter to his brother in Vienna, signing it Johann van Beethoven, landowner. *Beethoven wrote back, signing his letter* Ludwig van Beethoven, brain owner.

When, many years earlier, Beethoven had heard Johann intended marrying his housekeeper, a certain Therese Obermayer, he rushed to the city of Linz in central Austria, where Johann ran a pharmacy, and confronted his brother:

You want to marry your housekeeper?! Give the name "Beethoven" to a housekeeper?! I have one brother married to an immoral woman, I am not allowing the other to marry a housekeeper!

For good measure he added that Therese was not just a housekeeper, but deeply immoral too (like Carl's wife Johanna). She had an illegitimate child, which Johann – to Beethoven's increased horror – was prepared to adopt.

I have some fascinating and hitherto unpublished information about this child. All will be revealed in Chapter 10, The Last Master.

Beethoven approached the local bishop in Linz, and then the local police, insisting, pleading with them to stop his brother marrying Therese. They waved him away.

On 8 November 1812 Johann married Therese Obermayer, to whom he was still married nearly 14 years later when Beethoven, in failing health, arrived at their country estate with nephew Karl, head still bandaged from the bullet wound.

You can only imagine what the atmosphere inside that house must have been like.

Beethoven was a little unkind in considering his brother to be a complete fool. True, Johann mortgaged himself to the hilt to buy a pharmacy in Linz, and was in danger of defaulting on repayments. But a year after buying it, Austria declared war on France, and Napoleon Bonaparte marched his army to the gates of Vienna, shelled the city and occupied it. Where did he establish his base camp? Outside Linz. Who won contracts to provide medicine, bandages, splints, and so on?

And so Johann accumulated a considerable fortune, which he used to buy the estate at Gneixendorf. He also acquired the

It went wrong from the start. Johann gave Beethoven a set of small rooms which he loathed and said were far too cold.

These rooms are there to be seen today. See Chapter 10, The Last Master.

Then, to Beethoven's profound shock, Johann suggested he should move in on a more permanent basis – but at a price. Board and lodging for 40 florins a month. Beethoven was appalled, and refused.

Therese gave the cook the added duty of making Beethoven's bed. One day she was carrying this out, while Beethoven sat at a table, waving his arms in the air, muttering and singing. The poor woman

could not restrain herself and burst out laughing. Beethoven banned her from his rooms.

highly unenviable reputation of having collaborated with the enemy.

Of the three Beethoven brothers, Johann was the only one with absolutely no musical talent whatsoever (a possible cause of Beethoven's antagonism towards him). Long after his famous brother's death, Johann was to be seen at performances of his music, "all got up in a blue frock coat with white waistcoat, loudly shrieking Bravos from his big mouth at the end of every piece, clapping his bony white-gloved hands together importantly."

Locals soon became accustomed to the famous and eccentric composer striding across the fields, shouting and waving his arms, stopping to jot something down in a notebook. At first, not knowing who he was, they took him to be a madman. Then word got around.

The tensions in the house were palpable – all emanating from Beethoven. There was the added factor that he was concerned Karl was becoming idle. Karl himself was able to exploit the situation, standing up more to his uncle Ludwig, as if the suicide attempt had given him courage. In a major victory he secured his uncle's agreement for him to enter the army.

On one occasion a farmer, driving a pair of oxen, came upon this "madman" waving his arms and shouting. The oxen took fright and stampeded down a hill. The farmer ran after them and managed to bring them under control. Too late, there was the "madman" again, still shouting and gesticulating. The farmer shouted at him, but to no avail. The oxen took off again, to be stopped further down the path by another peasant. The farmer asked the peasant who the fool was who had scared his oxen, and was told he was the brother of the owner of the estate up the hill. Fine brother, that's all I can say, *was the response.*

Johann took Beethoven with him into town one day, where he had to meet an official on business. The meeting lasted some time. Beethoven stood silently at the door of the office for the whole time, saying nothing. After the brothers had left, the official turned to his clerk, whom he knew to be an admirer of Beethoven's music:

Official   *Who do you think that man was who stood by the door?*

Given the atmosphere in the house, it is surprising Beethoven and Karl stayed for as long as they did – two full months.

On a cold wet day, 1 December 1826, Beethoven made a sudden decision to return to Vienna. His health was now dreadful and he wanted to see his own doctor. He told Johann he needed the covered carriage and a servant to drive him and Karl back to Vienna.

Clerk	*From the deference you accorded him, I would imagine someone important. Otherwise I would have taken him for an imbecile.*
Official	*That was Beethoven.*
Clerk	*[dumbstruck]*

There is yet another anecdote that Johann took Beethoven with him to visit a friend, a doctor, but who happened to be out on a sick call. The doctor's wife, flattered to have the landowner Johann van Beethoven in her house, entertained him lavishly. Then she noticed the shabby withdrawn man sitting silently on a bench behind the stove.

Taking him for a servant, she said: "He shall have a drink too," and handed him a small jug of the roughest wine she had. When the doctor returned and his wife explained what had happened, he said: "My dear wife, what have you done? The greatest composer of the century was in our house today and you treated him with such disrespect!"

Who can blame Johann for extracting a small piece of revenge on his tempestuous brother? *I am not giving you the covered carriage. You shall have to use the open one.*

Beethoven later told his doctor he and Karl travelled in the most wretched vehicle of the devil, a milk wagon.

189

Pity, pity, too late

They stayed the night in an inn shortly after crossing the Danube. Beethoven's room had storm windows which did not shut properly. In the night he fell seriously ill. When he came down the next morning the landlord took one look at him and shooed him and Karl off the premises as quickly as he could.

By the time Beethoven reached his apartment in Vienna, he was in a dreadful state. His stomach was hugely swollen, he had a fever, a hacking cough, and sharp pains in his sides. He occasionally spat blood. His strength seemed to have gone out of his body.

His doctor was summoned. Problem. A couple of years earlier, after repeatedly refusing to follow his doctor's orders, he had insulted the man in front of others. Exit Dr Jakob Staudenheim. When the call came to attend Beethoven, Staudenheim refused to come.

Another of his doctors was called. Problem. Only the previous year, despite such confidence in him that Beethoven had penned a little canon for him, he had then totally lost confidence in him and described him as a *crazy man*. And so Dr Anton Braunhofer, too, refused to come.

A third doctor was called, but was himself sick. The doctor who finally attended Beethoven had never met him before, knew nothing of his medical history, and found himself caring for the most famous artist in Europe.

A lesser doctor might have flinched. But Dr Andreas Wawruch, a highly respected physician, quickly realized the gravity of the situation. He diagnosed dropsy, and recommended a range of concoctions as well as plenty of water with cream of tartar and sugar added.

Dropsy is an archaic medical term which essentially means an excess of fluid within a tissue.

Wawruch visited Beethoven every day, and was pleased to see that on the seventh day Beethoven was able to get up, walk about, read and write. On the eighth day everything changed:

At the morning visit I found him in great physical distress, jaundiced over his whole body. A terrible vomiting and diarrhoea attack had struck him in the night, so violent it threatened his life. A violent rage, a deep hurt from ingratitude suffered and undeserved insult induced the powerful explosion. Shivering and trembling, he writhed with pains which raged in the liver and bowels, and his hitherto only moderately bloated feet were massively swollen.

A violent rage and a deep hurt . . . Wawruch is too tactful to enlighten us further. It seems there was some kind of trauma in the night, probably involving Karl who was preparing to leave to join his regiment, that catastrophically worsened Beethoven's condition.

The dropsy was taking hold. Beethoven's stomach was still dreadfully swollen and Wawruch suspected his patient was developing acute inflammation of the liver. Something needed to be done immediately.

Wawruch summoned the Chief Surgeon at Vienna General Hospital, Johann Seibert. He decided to drain Beethoven's stomach. He made an incision in Beethoven's side (no anaesthetics, remember) and inserted a tube into the abdomen. The fluid gushed out. The relief must have been instantaneous, because Beethoven made a joke:

Professor, you remind me of Moses striking the rock with his staff!

Fluid oozed from Beethoven's side for days, but his stomach was filling up again faster than it was emptying. Nineteen days later Seibert performed the procedure again. Yet more fluid was drawn off than before, and Seibert was encouraged to note that it was clearer than the first time.

Then something quite extraordinary happened. Beethoven's favourite doctor of all re-entered the scene. This was a certain Dr Johann Malfatti, who had treated Beethoven for several years, before Beethoven decided he was nothing more than an incompetent and crafty Italian and sacked him.

Malfatti. Sound familiar? Yes, uncle of Therese Malfatti, the pupil with whom Beethoven had fallen in love and for whom he had composed the Bagatelle *known to the world as* Für Elise.

Did Beethoven, who (true to form) was becoming disillusioned with Wawruch, summon him, or did Malfatti himself, hearing his old patient was *in extremis*, decide to come? We do not know.

What we *do* know is that Malfatti, while taking great pains not to tread on Wawruch's toes, in effect said to him: *Look, the man is dying. It's obvious. There is only one thing that will bring him relief. Alcohol. Let him drink. What harm can it do, other than hasten the inevitable? At least it will make him happy.*

Wawruch agreed, and so Beethoven was given frozen fruit punch to drink. And do you know what? Malfatti was right. Beethoven's mood improved. He made sketches for a new symphony. He began to believe the impossible. He began to believe he would get better. And so he drank more. And more. And more . . .

On 2 February 1827 Seibert drained Beethoven's stomach for a third time. The wound in his side was now infected. Only the fruit punch eased the searing pain in his head as Seibert inserted the tube.

It was obvious to everyone that the end was approaching. Everyone except Beethoven, who wrote to the wine merchant Schott's, asking them to send him some Rhine or Mosel wine. He then wrote to the Philharmonic Society of London, thanking them for their gift of £100, and offering to compose a new symphony for them. And all the time he continued work on that new symphony, making sketches for his tenth.

At the end of February, yes, Seibert inserted that tube for a fourth time, after which everyone agreed it was pointless to do it – or anything else – again.

Some days after this, after the medical team had held a long and grave consultation at his bedside, Beethoven said in a tone described as *sarcastic-humorous*:

Plaudite, amici, comedia finita est.

Which tells us, if nothing else, he had finally accepted the inevitable. Around 22 March he received the last rites – more at the instigation of those around him than of his own volition, though

194

as the priest left, Beethoven said (and again his unusual form of address suggests, I believe, a sarcastic humour in the remark):

I am most grateful, holy one. You have really brought me comfort!

On 24 March the shipment of wine from Schott's arrived. Everyone agrees on what Beethoven said:

Pity, pity. Too late.

Those were his last words.

He fell into a coma that lasted for two days. In the late afternoon of 26 March 1827 a storm blew up over Vienna. At 5.45 pm there was a crashing roar of thunder. Beethoven opened his eyes, raised his arm, fist clenched, and sank back.

The boy whose talent had first revealed itself to the world on a stage in Cologne on 26 March 1778 left the world, its most famous and revered artist, on the same day 49 years later.

The Last Master

You can walk in Beethoven's footsteps today.

A Very Picture of Neatness and Comfort

Let us begin where he began – in the small, neat, sophisticated, and wealthy little town on the banks of the majestic Rhine, where the Elector of Cologne, member of the illustrious and imperial family of the Holy Roman Emperor, had his palace, and which owed its existence – and continued importance – to the geographical accident that the Rhine narrows at this point so that in time of war it could be blockaded.

A town where the tiny population of under 10,000 souls practically all derived employment in one form or another from service to the Elector; where a partially destroyed city wall still served to maintain a certain exclusivity within; where away from the river the nobility held court, while on its bank a constant bustle of barges, loading and unloading, dotted the landing stage, as other boats, drawn by sails, horses or even men, plied the water; where a single large ferryboat zigzagged across the current . . .

. . . A town a short distance, but a world apart, from its mighty neighbours:

To the stranger coming down from Mainz, with its narrow dark lanes, or up from Cologne, whose confined and filthy plague-filled streets emitted an unmentionable stench, both cities typical of the bigotry, superstition and moral filth of the population, little Bonn seemed a very picture of neatness and comfort.

Beethoven could not have chosen a more suitable place to be born, nor a more fitting milieu in the whole of the Holy Roman Empire for his unique talent to flower.

Despite its elevated status, royalty and nobility, and despite its later unexpected choice as the capital of an artificially divided country, Bonn has never produced any person or anything that comes even close to Beethoven. He remains its most famous son.

The small house in the *Bonngasse* owned by Clasen the lace maker, at the back of which Johann van Beethoven rented two small attic rooms and one larger one, and in which their son Ludwig was born (according to legend in one of the attic rooms), is – incredibly – still there. It was bought by the Beethoven Society only in 1889. The fact that it had not been destroyed or demolished in the turbulent century since the Beethovens left it is nothing short of a miracle, particularly since an inn was opened on the ground floor in 1873 and a beer and concert hall added a few years later in the courtyard.

It is, of course, today a shrine for millions of Beethoven enthusiasts from across the world. In recent years it has been restored, and contains a wealth of original material. When I first visited the house 20 or so years ago, a table under the staircase was spread with some cassettes and a few research articles. Now, next door, is an extensive souvenir shop, selling everything from tacky Beethoven T-shirts and mugs to highly academic books.

Also next door is the Beethoven-Archiv, which houses the most valuable collection of autograph manuscripts and letters anywhere in the world. Again, two decades ago this was just a number of rooms with a small library. Now it is an entire building, with a concert hall for chamber music, and a wealth of material available online at its website, **www.beethoven-haus-bonn.de**.

It also has the original life mask taken by the sculptor Franz Klein in 1812, from which he modelled his famous bust. The life mask is kept in a sealed glass cabinet at a constant temperature. It is, obviously, the most accurate representation that exists of Beethoven's features.

Have a look at the little house now by visiting the website and clicking on Museum/Virtual visit. You can take a tour of the house, and view the exterior via a webcam which gives you a live picture, refreshed every minute – and you'll see the freshly painted and neat-as-a-picture house as the Beethoven family (and the other families who squeezed into it) certainly did not know it!

The most important research centre outside Europe is the Center for Beethoven Studies at the University of San José, California, endowed by a former student and lifelong Beethoven devotee who made a fortune in property development. Painstakingly the dedicated staff at the Center are cataloguing everything of significance ever written about Beethoven. To date over 4000 books, articles and documents have been catalogued. It is, of course, a never ending process. Visit their website at www2.sjsu.edu/depts/beethoven and marvel.

The Bonn house where Beethoven spent most of his childhood and teenage years – the Fischer house in the *Rheingasse* – has long since gone. There's no mistaking where it once stood: in its place today an

unprepossessing modern hotel with not a single
relevant picture or artefact (nor, when I visited it,
a receptionist who had the first idea as to the
relevance of the location or name), just a garish sign
outside, *Hotel Beethoven*.

City of Music

I have on my wall at home a map of Vienna
published in 1827, the year in which Beethoven
died. Stand in front of it with today's map of
Vienna, and you will be surprised at how little has
changed – despite two Napoleonic invasions and
two world wars.

The most notable change is that the great city
wall, the *Bastei*, built to defend Vienna from the
Turks, was pulled down in the 1850s and replaced
by the wide boulevards known today as the
Ringstrassen. Inside the *Ringstrassen* the city is
much as it was two centuries ago. Beethoven
could walk round the inner city today and know
exactly where he was. Let us take a little walk
with him.

He turns quickly off the *Kärntnerstrasse*, ignoring
the Malfatti house where he embarrassed himself
over the *Bagatelle* for Therese, into the
Himmelpfortgasse. There he steps into the *Café
Frauenhuber*, which he knew as the *Café Jahn*, has a
coffee or a glass of red wine, and remembers how he

first performed his *Opus 16 Quintet for Piano and Wind* in the music room upstairs.

Leaving the *Frauenhuber*, he crosses the *Himmelpfortgasse* into the *Rauhensteingasse*. Looking up at the first-floor windows behind which, in the early hours of a December morning, the great Wolfgang Amadeus died, and no doubt bowing his head in respect, he walks on to the next corner on the right. This is exactly where the house stood in which his brother Carl died.

No lingering, too many bad memories, so he turns down the *Ballgasse*, and, yes, there it is, today just as it was two centuries ago, the "Zum alten Blumenstock". Rubbing his hands in anticipation, he strides straight to the small table at the back that he had made his own: *Bring me red wine, keep the carafe full, and fish, my favourite dish.*

The half-day's coach ride north to the little village of Heiligenstadt, at the foot of the hills of the Vienna Woods, is today a 10-minute ride on the *U-Bahn*. Once there, though, he immediately recognizes the small house in which he wrote his Last Will and Testament, acknowledging for the first time his deafness. Restored to its original condition, complete with exterior wooden staircase, it is easy to imagine it as a small country cottage providing escape from the city.

Point out to him that the walk he so often took to the foot of the *Kahlenberg* is now named the *Eroicagasse*, that the path by the stream that gave him the inspiration for the second movement of the *Pastoral Symphony* is now the *Beethovengang*, and show him the bust of himself mounted on a pedestal standing at the end of it . . . and he nods as if expecting nothing less.

Don't let him leave without showing him what I believe is the most accurate representation of him ever created. By St Michael's church in Heiligenstadt there stands a full-size statue of Beethoven. He is walking, hands clasped behind his back, long frockcoat flapping open. Unlike every portrait and every other statue or bust of Beethoven, all of which portray him as some sort of god, this is Beethoven the man. All right, the hair may be a touch too neat, the coat a little smarter than he was used to. But this *is* Beethoven. Amazing, then, that it was sculpted in 1902, and not from life. Perhaps the passage of time allowed the sculptor, one Robert Weigl, to separate the man from the myth.

He will refuse point blank to go there – again, too many bad memories – but in the village of Gneixendorf, two or three hours' drive from Vienna, west along the Danube, stands his brother Johann's country estate; on the first floor, the small self-contained apartment in which Beethoven stayed. Even allowing for the passage of time, it is beautiful – he had no right to complain!

The family who now own the house, and produce and bottle local wine, are well used to Beethoven enthusiasts beating a path to their door, and are proud to show you round, pointing out that everything in the small apartment is either original or of the period.

To stand in these rooms, gazing at the furniture he knew, seeing the murals he saw, is to bring you as close to Beethoven as you will ever come.

"You Damned Fool"

Beethoven is never out of the news. Whether it is a manuscript at auction, a letter discovered, or scientific research, barely a week goes by without a mention in the newspapers – not including performances of his music and reviews.

On 22 May 2003 the only complete score of the *Ninth Symphony* known to exist, the manuscript which establishes the definitive text of one of the greatest musical works ever written, the manuscript from which Beethoven almost certainly "conducted" at that famous first performance when Karoline Unger turned him round to face the cheering audience . . . in other words, 575 hand-written pages whose importance surpasses anything

words can express, sold at auction in London for
£2.1 million.

A pittance. Attendance was sparse and the bidding
was very, very slow, reaching nowhere near the
expected £3 million. Why? Because, quite simply, the
pages were written by two scribes, not Beethoven.

*Only the year before a single sheet of an early draft of the
opening of the first movement* in Beethoven's hand *sold for
£1.5 million, eight times more than the estimated price.*

The neatness alone gives that away at a mere casual
glance. But Beethoven's hand *is* on the manuscript.
He writes the occasional word of instruction –
Recitativo and *Ritmo di tre Battute.*

But here – for me – is the most delicious feature of
the whole manuscript. At one point in this work,
which, let us remember, is the seminal testament to
universal brotherhood and love, Beethoven, fed up
with the copyist's mistakes, writes in the margin:

Du verfluchter Kerl [You damned fool]

That's my Beethoven.

Who knows what surprises are in store for us in
future years? In 1999 a hitherto unknown
composition by Beethoven, a short single string
quartet movement, *written in his hand,* was

found . . . in a stately home near Bodmin in Cornwall! In December 2003 the working score of the entire *Scherzo* movement of the first of the *Late Quartets*, again in Beethoven's hand, was put up for auction, allowing us to see crossings out and scribblings so furious you can easily imagine him storming about the room, hearing the sounds in his head, frustrated beyond measure at the difficulty in getting his pen to transfer the sounds to paper.

Most recently, and most extraordinarily, in October 2005 a librarian at an evangelical seminary near Philadelphia was cleaning out a dirty cabinet in the building's basement. There, hidden away on a bottom shelf, was a dusty old book covered in striped paper. She carefully opened it, and found herself looking at Beethoven's hand:

I thought, Wow! I was just in a state of shock.

The manuscript was Beethoven's own version of his mighty *Grosse Fuge* string quartet movement arranged for piano four-hands, dating from 1826, the last complete year of his life. The manuscript, known about in the 19th century, had been lost for 115 years. And, as this is Beethoven, alongside the furiously scribbled notes, there are smudges where he wiped away wet ink, holes in the paper where he tried to rub notes out, and the word aus [out]. No one listening to the *Grosse Fuge*, a work which drains performers and audience alike, will be surprised at that.

> *I once heard those supreme Beethoven performers, The Lindsays, perform the* Grosse Fuge *at London's Wigmore Hall. At the end, as they rose to take applause, their leader, Peter Cropper, was white-faced, blood-drained, shirt dark with sweat, gripping the back of his chair to maintain his balance. I thought he might fall as he walked off stage.*

Before World War Two, most existing Beethoven manuscripts were held in the Prussian State Library, but in 1945 the collection was split into three and housed in West Berlin, East Berlin and Krakow. Manuscripts of some of the most important works are still missing. Some, certainly, are lost for ever. But who knows . . . ?

> *In my dreams I walk into an antiquarian bookseller somewhere in central Europe, peruse a few dusty books, and there staring at me in Beethoven's hand are the great opening chords of the* Eroica Symphony, *that changed the course of music for ever.*

And letters. Ah! Letters. Remember the 13 letters to Josephine Brunsvik that only came to light in 1949? And the young woman whose mother has a shoebox in the attic . . . ?

So who knows?

DNA

I mentioned the strands of hair and fragments of skull in *Chapter 5, I Am Deaf.*

The day after Beethoven's death, so many admirers had come to pay their respects, and indulged in the traditional practice of cutting off a lock of hair as a memento, that – according to one eyewitness – Beethoven had lost all his hair.

One hundred and sixty-seven years later a single lock, containing 582 strands, was purchased at auction by the American Beethoven Society. Of these strands, 160 were subjected to DNA testing in the USA.

There were two crucial findings. The first, as I have already described in *I Am Deaf,* was that the absence of mercury proved that Beethoven did not have syphilis.

The second, more importantly, showed that the levels of lead in his blood when he died were around 100 times higher than we today would consider normal. Why might this be? Well, we know that he used heavy lead pencils to write music, and he might well have sucked on them. All kitchen utensils in those days were made of lead. Paint was lead-based.

We would say today that Beethoven had lead poisoning. But that is not to say he *died* of lead poisoning. It certainly exacerbated conditions he already had, but it did not kill him, and is unlikely to have affected his deafness. There is a further point to consider: what about other people of the time? Did they too have the same levels of lead in their blood? We do not know, for the simple reason that their hair has not been tested. It is quite likely that *most* people had some degree of lead poisoning.

So, while the discovery of the lead poisoning is interesting, helping us to fill in certain details, that is all it is.

But one day, 50 years from now, 100 years, 200, some of those remaining strands will be tested. And, as I said earlier, I am convinced the world will then know what caused his deafness. And if they do not at that point give up their secret, then in another 50 years, or 100, or 200, more strands will be tested. One day we will know. And it will be front-page news.

It might come sooner than we think, thanks to those skull fragments I mentioned earlier. Although the DNA testing on the hair strands gave us important information, it was unable to give us the full sequence of Beethoven's DNA.

But bone fragments are more reliable than hair strands. As I write this, those skull fragments are undergoing tests. First of all, of course, they must be authenticated, which means matching them with the hair. Then the detailed and minute testing can begin.

Keep an eye on those front pages.

Scoop!

In the *Introduction* to this book I promised you revelations about Beethoven and those close to him that have never been published before. Time to keep that promise.

Revenge for Murder

Soon after I established my Beethoven website, www.madaboutbeethoven.com, in February 2000, I received an email from a gentleman with a very familiar surname. *Razumovsky*.

Anyone familiar with Beethoven's music will have heard of Beethoven's *Razumovsky Quartets*. In 1806 Count Andrei Razumovsky, Russian ambassador to the Austrian court – music lover, artistic patron, amateur violinist, and without doubt one of the most influential figures in the social and musical life of Vienna – commissioned Beethoven to compose a set of string quartets.

That much is common knowledge. Less well-known is the glittering – and ultimately tragic – life the count led.

Razumovsky was far more interested in music and the arts than he was in diplomacy. With his own money, bolstered by funds from the Tsar (as I believed when I wrote my website), he built a magnificent palace on the banks of the Danube, housing an amazing library and fabulous art collection containing several Canova sculptures. He maintained his own string quartet, in which he frequently played second violin.

For his efforts representing his country at the Congress of Vienna in 1814 he was elevated to the rank of prince. On New Year's Eve of that year he held a glittering ball at his palace with Tsar Alexander as guest of honour.

To accommodate all the guests, he had a temporary extension built onto the palace, heated from the main building by a flue. Some time in the early hours of the morning – New Year's Day 1815 – a fire started in the flue and spread rapidly to the main house.

Razumovsky joined the efforts to stop the flames spreading. But little could be done. They engulfed the building, destroying many of the rooms, along with the art treasures they contained.

At daybreak Razumovsky was found wandering in the ruins, his eyesight irreparably damaged by the smoke and flames, and his spirit broken.

The Tsar assured Razumovsky he would contribute to the reconstruction of the palace, but the money was never forthcoming. The prince retired from the Russian diplomatic corps. He lived on in Vienna, a virtual recluse, until his death 22 years later.

That much I knew. Then I received that email from an executive consultant in Vienna by the name of Gregor Razumovsky. With extreme politeness he wished to draw to my attention the fact that the Tsar had contributed no money at all to the building of his ancestor's sumptuous palace. Count Razumovsky himself had financed the entire project. Furthermore, the Tsar had refused to make a financial contribution to the reconstruction of the palace after the disastrous fire.

There was a reason for this. The Tsar, Herr Razumovsky informed me, held a deep personal hatred for his ambassador, whom he suspected of having supported the assassination of his father, Tsar Paul. And so, *for good reason* (writes Gregor Razumovsky), the Tsar never kept his word.

We can therefore conclude that the man whose name will live for ever thanks to his good fortune in knowing a certain Ludwig van Beethoven, was

almost certainly involved, albeit passively, in the murder of the Russian Tsar.

Great-great-great-great . . .

Your starter for 10: what is the connection between Beethoven and a London police officer?

Remember Therese Obermayer? She was housekeeper to Johann van Beethoven in Linz. When Johann announced he was to marry her, his brother rushed to Linz to try to stop the marriage. His main objection: she had an illegitimate child.

I promised you exclusive information about that illegitimate child. Once again, it came unexpectedly as a result of my website.

I received an email from a certain Adrian Hay, first of all thanking me for devoting a whole page to the largely forgotten Therese Obermayer, and then providing me with historical family details that I confess took my breath away.

That illegitimate daughter was christened Amalia and was given the surname of Therese's mother, Waldmann, possibly to avoid embarrassment to the Obermayer family. The father's name was left blank on the birth certificate, and alongside Amalia's name is the cruel word *unehelich* [illegitimate].

Therese, Adrian informed me, was in no position to look after her daughter, and Amalia was placed first in a foster home and then in an orphanage.

It was in the next few years that Therese, needing to earn money, made a decision that ensured her a certain immortality. She became housekeeper to Johann van Beethoven in Linz. The professional relationship soon turned to romance, and on 8 November 1812 – despite Beethoven's best efforts – they married. Johann – to his brother's further disgust and anger – agreed to have Amalia to live with them.

On 11 February 1830, at the age of 23, Amalia married a forester by the name of Karl Stölzle. Amalia gave birth to a son later in the same year, but four months later she died, possibly due to complications following the birth.

Amalia's son – Therese's grandson, Johann van Beethoven's step-grandson – went on to have 10 children of his own. The eldest, Gustav, came to England, married an English woman, Elizabeth Wallis, in London, and had three children, two sons and a daughter.

Ironically the two sons both died fighting for the Allies in the world wars, the eldest with the Royal Engineers in World War One, the youngest as an RAF pilot shot down over Germany in 1941.

The daughter, Doris Anna, who died in Cumbria in 1978, was grandmother to my correspondent Adrian Hay.

Adrian is therefore great-great-great grandson of the illegitimate daughter of the woman who married Beethoven's brother. And yes, you guessed it, he is a police officer with the Met!

Shock!

The biggest surprise of all again came totally out of the blue, not this time via email. I had just given my Beethoven talk at a private function in west London, and was meeting various members of the audience. A tall, distinguished-looking woman in her 70s came up to me and introduced herself as Lady Chelwood, widow of the late Conservative MP Sir Tufton Beamish. After his retirement from the Commons, she explained, he had entered the Lords as Baron Chelwood of Lewes.

I detected the very slightest foreign accent in her otherwise totally fluent English. She then said she had been particularly interested in my story about the *Moonlight Sonata* and Giulietta Guicciardi. She continued:

Did you know that Giulietta went on to marry a man by the name of Count Gallenberg?

215

I confessed that I did. *A mediocre musician,* I said, *who went with Giulietta to live in Italy.*

Yes, but did you know Gallenberg was impotent?

My jaw dropped. I did not know.

Yes, Gallenberg was impotent. Because of that, he allowed Giulietta to take a lover, by the name of Count Schulenberg. With Schulenberg Giulietta had five illegitimate children, a son and four daughters. The son is my great-great-grandfather.

She explained that Gallenberg formally adopted the son and eldest daughter, giving them his mother's maiden name, *von Roretz*. She told me her own maiden name was, therefore, *von Roretz*, although strictly speaking she was a *Schulenberg*. Maria Schulenberg.

Call me Pia. It's what I've been called since I was a child.

She went on to tell me that Giulietta was regarded as the black sheep of the family for having illegitimate children (perhaps because she went on to have three more illegitimate children after her husband adopted the first two). Pia's uncle would not allow Giulietta's name to be mentioned in the house.

My wife Bonnie and I have come to know Pia well, and have several times been guests at her beautiful house in West Sussex. There, in pride of place on a pedestal before the wide drawing room window, stands a white marble bust of Giulietta Guicciardi, done from life.

Whenever I see Pia, I have to pinch myself to remember I am talking to the great-great-great-granddaughter of the woman for whom Beethoven composed the *Moonlight Sonata*, with whom he fell in love, and to whom he proposed marriage.

The Story Continues . . .

There must be more. I know, for instance, that there is an English woman living in London who married a direct descendant of the Russian Prince Galitzin, who commissioned three of the *Late Quartets* from Beethoven.

I conclude with a question I have already asked so many times. Who knows what else, or who else, might come to light next month, next year, next decade, next century . . . ?

Have a Listen Yourself

Every year, our listeners vote for their favourite
three pieces of music in the Classic FM Hall of
Fame. Here, we have gathered together a list of
Beethoven's Top 20 works, as voted by Classic FM
listeners.

You will find excerpts of each of these pieces on
the CD which accompanies this book.
Hopefully, these tasty morsels will whet your
appetite for listening to more of the great
man's music. We have deliberately chosen all of
the excerpts from full-length CDs on the
Naxos label. All Naxos discs are released at a

budget price and represent excellent value for money, so you will quickly be able to build up a relatively inexpensive collection of Beethoven's greatest hits.

1 Piano Concerto No. 5 – The Emperor

When audiences first heard Beethoven's final piano concerto, they were amazed. This was the longest piano concerto ever to have been written at the time – far longer than anything that Mozart ever created for piano and orchestra. It was also composed by a man who was too deaf to be able to perform it in public himself. Beethoven was no longer a fan of Napoleon when he wrote this and so the nickname did not come from the composer's pen. Instead, so the story goes, when a member of the audience heard the majesty of this piece, he declared it to be an "Emperor of a Concerto".

CD Track 1 is an excerpt from the beginning of the 1st movement, taken from Naxos 8.550121. When you hear this, it is easy to understand how the work earned its nickname.

If you enjoy this, then try Beethoven's *Piano and Wind Quintet Opus 16* (Naxos 8.550511).

2 Symphony No. 6 – The Pastoral

In Beethoven's day concertgoers were certainly given value for money. This work was premiered at the same concert in 1808 that his *Symphony No.5*, *Piano Concerto No. 4* and *Choral Fantasy* all received their first public hearing. As you can read on pages 94–99, it was quite some occasion, for all the wrong reasons. This symphony is unusual because it has five movements, instead of four. Beethoven's music underlines his love of nature and each of the movements is given a subtitle: *The Awakening of Joyful Feelings Upon Arrival in the Country, Scene by the Brook, Joyous Gathering of Country Folk, The Storm* and *The Shepherds' Song of Thanksgiving*.

CD Track 2 is an excerpt from the final movement, *The Shepherds' Song of Thanksgiving*, taken from Naxos 8.553474.

If you enjoy this, then try Beethoven's *Piano Sonata No. 15*, which is also known as the *Pastoral* (Naxos 8.550255).

3 Symphony No. 9

First performed in Vienna in 1824, this piece was actually commissioned by the London (now Royal) Philharmonic Society. In its famous last movement,

Beethoven set to music Friedrich Schiller's *Ode to Joy* to create a choral masterpiece. Another extraordinarily long piece of music for the time, it set a new standard for symphonic composition.

CD Track 3 gives you the closing bars of the climax of the piece – the final movement. It is taken from Naxos 8.553478.

If you enjoy this, then try Beethoven's *Battle Symphony* (extracts on Naxos 8.550230).

4 Symphony No. 5

De-De-De-Derr. De-De-De-Derr. It's the most famous opening of any piece of classical music and over the years all sorts of theories have been put forward to explain the significance of those opening few bars. The most popular story has it that this is the sound of fate knocking on the door, although a less mystical explanation that has done the rounds is that it is in fact the sound of Beethoven's grumpy cleaner knocking to be let in. Whatever the truth, it makes for a cracking start to the symphony.

CD Track 4 is an excerpt from the very start of that 1st movement, taken from Naxos 8.553476.

If you enjoy this, then try Beethoven's *Symphony No. 2* (also on Naxos 8.553476).

5 Symphony No. 7

This is edge-of-the-seat stuff, with a driving rhythm throughout all four of the movements. It earned Beethoven plenty of money, which was just as well because life was not as great as it might have been when he wrote it. He was suffering more and more from both deafness and unrequited passion. To top it all, the Napoleonic wars were at their height.

CD Track 5 is from the end of the 2nd movement, which has a particularly memorable melody. It is taken from Naxos 8.553477.

If you enjoy this, then try Beethoven's *Symphony No. 4* (also on Naxos 8.553477).

6 Piano Sonata No. 14 (The Moonlight)

Another nickname that was not given by the composer himself. Instead, it was a critic who first heard the work while he was looking out at the moonlight reflecting on the waters of Lake Lucerne. This is not a complicated piece to play, but it conveys huge amounts of emotion when it is performed by a pianist with real talent. This work is notable in that it starts with its slow movement, rather than having it in the middle, as was the norm.

CD Track 6 is the beginning of that 1st slow movement, taken from Naxos 8.550045.

If you enjoy this, then try Beethoven's *Piano Sonata No. 26 "Les Adieux"* (Naxos 8.550054).

7 Violin Concerto

This may have been the only violin concerto that Beethoven wrote, but he proved himself to be a master of the genre. This was all the more remarkable a feat as he was himself a pianist, rather than a string player. It was not, however, an instant hit, only becoming part of the mainstream violin repertoire in the second half of the 19th century.

CD Track 7 gives you the opening of the 3rd movement, where the solo violin is given the opportunity to show us their mettle. It is taken from Naxos 8.550149.

If you enjoy this, then try Beethoven's *Violin Sonata No. 9 "Kreutzer"* (Naxos 8.550283).

8 Symphony No. 3 – The Eroica

This piece was written by Beethoven as a tribute to Napoleon, whom the composer admired greatly. That all changed, though, when Napoleon decided to crown himself Emperor. Beethoven didn't

approve in the slightest and he tore up the page of the manuscript that bore the original dedication. When the work was published, the dedication simply read "To the memory of a great man".

CD Track 8 is the beginning of the 2nd movement, taken from Naxos 8.553475. It was the first time that a funeral march had appeared in a symphony.

If you enjoy this, then try Beethoven's *Symphony No. 1* (Naxos 8.553474).

9 Romance No. 2 for Violin and Orchestra

Beethoven was starting to become very agitated by his advancing deafness when he wrote this piece – one of a pair of *Romances*. It contains a very beautiful melody and the whole piece only runs for 10 minutes in its entirety. The brevity may well be because Beethoven was using the two *Romances* as a sort of warm-up for writing his *Violin Concerto*.

CD Track 9 is an excerpt taken from Naxos 8.550149.

If you enjoy this, then try Beethoven's *Romance No. 1* (also on Naxos 8.550149).

10 Piano Concerto No. 4

There is a big difference in style and sound between Beethoven's third and fourth piano concertos. The piano opens the whole piece on its own, which was another revolutionary development at the time Beethoven composed the work.

CD Track 10 is the opening of the 2nd movement, which the composer Franz Liszt described as "Orpheus taming the wild beasts". It is taken from Naxos 8.550122.

If you enjoy this, then try Beethoven's *Piano Sonata No. 17 "Tempest"* (Naxos 8.550054).

11 Piano Sonata No. 8 (Pathétique)

The dictionary definition of "pathetic" which Beethoven intended us to infer was not the one meaning "exciting contempt"; rather, he intended the subtitle to convey a sense of pathos, something that evokes pity or sadness. As with the *Piano Concerto No. 3*, it is written in the key of C minor, which is perfect for underlining the sense of melancholy surrounding this beautiful piece.

CD Track 11 is the opening of the middle movement, which is in itself a love song. It is taken from Naxos 8.550045.

If you enjoy this, then try Beethoven's *Violin Sonata No. 5 "Spring"* (Naxos 8.550283).

12 Egmont Overture

Beethoven regularly composed incidental music for use in the theatre productions of the day. This particular overture came from the beginning of the incidental music he wrote for a new production of a play by Johann Wolfgang von Goethe, the German poet and playwright. There are nine other movements, but the overture is the only part of this work that is often played today.

CD Track 12 is the opening of the overture, taken from Naxos 8.550072.

If you enjoy this, then try Beethoven's *Coriolan Overture* (also on Naxos 8.550072).

13 Bagatelle No. 25 in A minor (Für Elise)

Beethoven wrote 26 of these *Bagatelles* or "trifles". The penultimate has become one of the best-known piano pieces of all time, not least because it is taught to children who learn to play the piano the world over. The original dedication is not actually "Für Elise" (literally "for Elise") at all. It is in fact "Für Therese" – a nameless individual made their mark on musical history by copying out the name wrongly. See pages 137–140 for more on this story.

CD Track 13 gives us the opening. It is taken from Naxos 8.553795.

If you enjoy this, then try Beethoven's *Rondo a capriccio (Rage over a lost penny)* (Naxos 8.550219).

14 Piano Concerto No. 3

This work has a stormy start to its 1st movement, before things calm down in the second section. The final movement has a more cheery and optimistic air to it. Experts say that Beethoven was paying homage to the style of concerto that his predecessors such as Mozart had been composing. At the same time, this piece crosses over from the style of the Classical era into what was to become the Romantic period.

CD Track 14 is the opening of the 2nd movement, which remains the most popular part of the work. It is taken from Naxos 8.550122.

If you enjoy this, then try Beethoven's *Piano Sonata No. 29 "Hammerklavier"* (Naxos 8.550234).

15 Piano Concerto No. 1

Now, don't get confused here, but Beethoven's *Piano Concerto No. 1* was actually the second piano

concerto that he composed, with his *Piano Concerto No. 2* being composed several years earlier. Both concertos were published in the same year, 1801, but by different publishers. The later concerto actually came out a few months before the earlier one, and so *Piano Concerto No. 2* is really the first one, and *Piano Concerto No. 1* is really the second. If you're still confused, just sit back and listen to the music.

CD Track 15 is the opening of the final movement, taken from Naxos 8.550190.

If you enjoy this, then try Beethoven's *Piano Concerto No. 2* (Naxos 8.550121).

16 Triple Concerto for Violin, Cello and Piano

Beethoven composed this piece for Archduke Rudolf on piano and two of his paid musicians on violin and cello. It makes huge demands on all three soloists, as you can hear in the exciting final movement.

CD Track 16 is the ending of the final movement, taken from Naxos 8.554288.

If you enjoy this, then try Beethoven's *Piano Trio No. 7 "Archduke"* (Naxos 8.550949).

17 Fidelio ✓

Beethoven only wrote one opera. He started working on it in 1804 and finally finished it a decade later. It turned out that, although he was utterly brilliant at virtually everything else, writing for singers caused him nothing but creative suffering. He couldn't even get the opening right – with four different versions of the overture being churned out over the years. There was one particular aria that he rewrote almost 20 times. The first version of *Fidelio* flopped and it now stands at only two acts, rather than the original three. It tells the story of Leonore, whose husband, Florestan, has unfairly been thrown into jail. In the end, love conquers all and Leonore and Florestan are reunited. But after all the stresses and strains for Beethoven in its composition is the opera actually any good? Of course it is. A triumph, it is quite probably the greatest German opera ever written, although it remains the only example of the genre that Beethoven actually completed.

CD Track 17 is an excerpt from the "*Prisoners' Chorus*", taken from Naxos 8.660070–71.

If you enjoy this, then try Beethoven's ballet, *The Creatures of Prometheus* (Naxos 8.553404).

18 Symphony No. 8

This is by no means Beethoven's best-known symphony, often being overshadowed by the mighty *Symphony No. 9*, which followed it. It sounds as if Beethoven was letting his hair down a little when he was writing this. There is no question that it is the brightest and most fun of all of his symphonies.

CD Track 18 is the opening of the 2nd movement, which is the most playful of the four movements. It is taken from Naxos 8.553475.

If you enjoy this, then try Beethoven's *The Ruins of Athens* (Naxos 8.550072).

19 Missa Solemnis

This work is quite rightly regarded as one of the greatest pieces anywhere in the history of religious music. It is made up six sections: *Kyrie, Gloria, Credo, Sanctus, Benedictus* and *Agnus Dei*. It's by no means an easy piece to sing, but when it is performed well, the sound is simply magnificent.

CD Track 19 is an excerpt from the *Benedictus*, taken from Naxos 8.557060.

If you enjoy this, then try Beethoven's "*Die Ehre Gottes aus der Natur*", from *Six Songs, Opus 48* (Naxos 8.553751).

20 Piano Sonata No. 23 (Appassionata)

Beethoven himself believed this to be the greatest of all of his piano sonatas. It gained its nickname after he had died, but the passion is there to hear throughout – particularly in the stormy finale. It has the same sort of feel to it as his *Symphony No. 5*, but here all of that energy is channelled into just one instrument, rather than into the whole orchestra. It's powerful stuff.

CD Track 20 is an excerpt from the violent climax to the sonata, the ending of the last movement. It is taken from Naxos 8.550045.

If you enjoy this, then try Beethoven's *Piano Sonata No. 21 "Waldstein"* (Naxos 8.550054).

Beethoven's Movie Music

Beethoven's music has turned up in a wide range of different films. In some cases, such as *Howards End* or *Mr. Holland's Opus*, the choices might be expected. But the inclusion of his work in *George of the Jungle* or *Star Trek: The Insurrection* would probably raise a few eyebrows among classical music purists.

Those celebrated opening bars of Beethoven's *Symphony No. 5*, the beautifully evocative *Moonlight Sonata* and that hardy staple of childhood piano classes *Für Elise* seem to be among the most popular choices when film directors sit down to decide on the music they are going to use in their latest epic.

IMMORTAL BELOVED

One film deserves a special mention above all others. Released in 1994, it tells the story of Beethoven's life and death. Now, we don't suggest for a moment that the film provides a wholly accurate biography of the great man. It does, however, offer you the chance to hear some of his greatest music all in one place.

The plot centres on the letter which Beethoven wrote to that unidentified "immortal beloved". The film tells the story of the search to unmask the great love of his life.

Among the many pieces of Beethoven's music included in the film, you should listen out for:
Für Elise
Piano Sonata No. 8, 2nd movement
Piano Sonata No. 14, 1st movement
Symphony No. 5, 1st movement
Symphony No. 6, 4th movement
Symphony No. 7, 2nd movement
Symphony No. 9, 4th movement
Violin Concerto, 1st movement

This is a selection of other popular movies which have included Beethoven's music:

The Age of Innocence: Piano Sonata No. 8, 2nd
  movement
Before Sunrise: Piano Sonata No. 8, 3rd movement
Celebrity: Symphony No. 5, 1st movement
A Clockwork Orange: Symphony No. 9, 4th
  movement
Colonel Chabert: Piano Trio No. 5, 2nd movement
Crimson Tide: Piano Sonata No. 14
Cruel Intentions: Symphony No. 9, 4th movement
Dead Poets' Society: Piano Concerto No. 5, 2nd
  movement; *Symphony No. 9*, 4th movement
Fantasia: Symphony No. 5
Fearless: Für Elise; Piano Concerto No. 5, 3rd
  movement
Fight Club: Symphony No. 5, 4th movement
George of the Jungle: String Quartet, Opus 18, No. 6
Hard Target: Piano Sonata No. 23, 3rd movement
Hilary And Jackie: Piano Trio No. 7, "Archduke"
The Horse Whisperer: Cello Sonata No. 1
Howards End: Symphony No. 5, 3rd movement
Invincible: Piano Concerto No. 3
K-19 The Widowmaker: Piano Sonata No. 14
Kalifornia: Symphony No. 8, 2nd movement
The Lost World: Piano Sonata No. 8, 2nd movement
Love Potion No. 9: Symphony No. 5; Symphony No. 6
Madame Souzatska: Piano Sonata No. 23, 3rd
  movement
The Magic Bow: Violin Concerto
*The Man who Wasn't There: Piano Sonata No. 8;
  Piano Sonata No. 14; Piano Trio No. 7*
Misery: Piano Sonata No. 14, 1st movement

Mr. Holland's Opus: Symphony No. 7, 2nd movement
Mr. Jones: Symphony No. 9
My Life so Far: Für Elise; Piano Sonata No. 23; Symphony No. 5
Onegin: "Mir ist so wunderbar" from *Fidelio*
Patch Adams: Für Elise
The Pianist: Piano Sonata No. 14; Piano Concerto No. 3
Rosemary's Baby: Für Elise
Star Trek: Insurrection: Piano Sonata No. 8, 1st movement
The Talented Mr Ripley: Piano Quintet, 2nd movement

What the Others Said About Beethoven

Whenever a composer premieres their latest work, they may be hoping for bouquets – but sometimes they receive only brickbats, especially from minor composers. And Beethoven was no exception: Spohr savaged his later works. But whoever listens to Spohr's music now? The greats, of course, were in no doubt.

We have divided this selection of sayings about Beethoven into three sections: the good, the bad and, in the case of our final quotation, the just plain confused.

THE GOOD . . .

I occasionally play works by contemporary composers for two reasons. First to discourage the composer from writing any more and secondly to remind myself how much I appreciate Beethoven.

JASCHA HEIFETZ, VIOLINIST

Beethoven's 5th Symphony *is the most sublime noise that has ever penetrated the ear of man.*

NOVELIST E.M. FORSTER IN THE BOOK
"HOWARDS END"

Composers in the old days used to keep strictly to the main theme. But Beethoven varies the melody, harmony and rhythms so beautifully.

JOHANNES BRAHMS

Beyond Beethoven's 9th no forward step is possible, for it can be followed only by artistic perfection.

RICHARD WAGNER

Articulate art is higher than inarticulate nature.

GUSTAV MAHLER, AFTER CONDUCTING
BEETHOVEN'S "PASTORAL SYMPHONY"

238

Beethoven embraced the universe with the power of his spirit.

FRÉDÉRIC CHOPIN

Le grand sourd ["The great deaf one"]

HECTOR BERLIOZ

Beethoven's music is music about music.

FRIEDRICH NIETZSCHE, PHILOSOPHER

I believe in Bach, the Father, Beethoven, the Son and Brahms, the Holy Ghost of music.

HANS VON BÜLOW, CONDUCTOR

Beethoven is the great "lawgiver" of music.

WILHELM FURTWÄNGLER, CONDUCTOR

If anyone has conducted a Beethoven performance, and then doesn't have to go to an osteopath, then there's something wrong.

SIR SIMON RATTLE, CONDUCTOR

Gee! This'll make Beethoven.

WALT DISNEY, ON USING THE "PASTORAL SYMPHONY" IN THE ANIMATED FILM "FANTASIA"

THE BAD . . .

An orgy of vulgar noise.

LOUIS SPOHR TALKING ABOUT THE

5TH SYMPHONY

So ugly, in such bad taste, and in the conception of Schiller's Ode so cheap that I cannot even now understand how such a genius as Beethoven could write it down.

LOUIS SPOHR, THIS TIME ABOUT THE

9TH SYMPHONY (THE ODE TO JOY)

AND THE CONFUSED . . .

At the height of The Beatles' fame in 1964, Ringo Starr was asked at a press conference what he thought of Beethoven. His reply:

I love him, especially his poems.

Where to Find Out More

If our *Friendly Guide to Beethoven* has sparked an interest in you, then you may well want to find out more about the man as well as his music.

One of the best general books on the subject is *The Beethoven Compendium: A Guide to Beethoven's Life and Music* edited by Barry Cooper and published by Thames & Hudson. The great musicologist H.C. Robbins Landon wrote *Beethoven: His Life, Work and World* in the 1970s and it remains one of the best single volumes about all things Beethoven.

John Suchet has written a painstakingly researched
and highly gripping trilogy of books about
Beethoven's life. *The Last Master: Passion and Anger*
is followed by *The Last Master: Passion and Pain,*
with *The Last Master: Passion and Glory* ending the
series. These books are published in hardback by
Little, Brown and in paperback by Time Warner.
They bring Beethoven's life into sharp relief and
give a real sense of him being a real person, rather
than an aloof historical figure.

If you have a yearning to read as near contemporary
as possible an account of Beethoven's life, then try
to find a copy of Alexander Wheelock Thayer's *Life
of Beethoven.* Alexander Wheelock Thayer was an
American who spent the best part of the second half
of the 19th century in Bonn and Vienna,
interviewing everyone he could find who had
known Beethoven. An edition of his work (edited
by Elliot Forbes) was published in 1964 by
Princeton University Press.

For a more general overview of classical music, *The
DK Eyewitness Companion to Classical Music,*
edited by John Burrows, provides an excellent and
very detailed journey through classical music from
its earliest beginnings to the present day. If you're
looking for something altogether more
quirky, then you might enjoy the Classic FM
book *Classic Ephemera,* published by Boosey &
Hawkes.

One of the best ways of keeping up to date with everything that is going on in the world of classical music is through the *Classic FM* magazine, which is published monthly with one, if not two, free CDs on the front cover. It contains a whole section of CD reviews, as does *The Gramophone*, the magazine that is regarded by many people as offering the definitive word on which CDs should be in your collection.

Of course there is no better way of getting closer to a composer than actually hearing his concerts live. Classic FM has a close relationship with the Royal Scottish National Orchestra, the Royal Liverpool Philharmonic Orchestra, the Philharmonia Orchestra and the London Symphony Orchestra. Beethoven's popularity is such that you can guarantee that these orchestras will perform some of his music at some stage during their season. For full listings of concerts near you, or to link through to our partner orchestras' websites, log on to **www.classicfm.com/events**.

While you are online, don't forget to check out John Suchet's own personal homage to the great man at www.madaboutbeethoven.com. For details of John's regular talks about Beethoven in theatres up and down the country, go to his personal website **www.johnsuchet.co.uk**.

If you are planning to make your journey of discovery of Beethoven's music an altogether more physical affair, then we would recommend trips to Bonn and Vienna. Make sure you keep copies of *The Rough Guide to Germany* by Gordon McLachlan and *Vienna: Eyewitness Travel Guide* by Stephen Brook to hand. To find out more about Austria in general, we recommend *The Rough Guide to Austria*, edited by Jonathan Bousfield and Rob Humphreys, and *Essential Austria*, by Des Harrison (part of the AA Essential Series).

Beethoven Mood Chart

Raise Your Blood Pressure

Lower Your Blood Pressure

The Creatures of Prometheus Overture

Bagatelle No. 25 in A minor (Für Elise)

Piano Concerto No. 4: 3rd mvt

Piano Concerto No. 5 (Emperor)- 3rd mvt

Piano Trio in Eb major: 2nd mvt

Piano Concerto No. 1: 3rd mvt

Piano Sonata No. 8 (Pathétique): 1st mvt

Piano Sonata No. 14 (Moonlight): 1st mvt

Symphony No. 5: 1st mvt

Symphony No. 3 (Eroica): 4th mvt

Piano Concerto No. 5: 2nd mvt

Piano Concerto No. 3: 3rd mvt

Egmont Overture

Piano Sonata No. 8 (Pathétique): 3rd mvt

Symphony No. 7: 4th mvt.

Piano Concerto No. 4: 3rd mvt

Symphony No. 5: 3rd mvt

Piano Sonata No. 8 (Pathétique): 2nd mvt

Romance No. 2 for violin & orch.

Symphony No. 6 (Pastoral): 1st mvt

Violin Sonata No. 5 (Spring): 3rd mvt

Symphony No. 6 (Pastoral): 2nd mvt

Symphony No. 6 (Pastoral): 4th mvt

Trio for clarinet, cello & piano in Bb: 2nd mvt

Symphony No. 8: 1st mvt

The Ruins of Athens Overture

Septet in Eb: 2nd mvt

Violin Concerto: 3rd mvt

Romance Cantabile in E minor for piano,
flute, bassoon & orch.: 2nd mvt

"Agnus Dei" from Mass in C major

Symphony No. 9 (Choral): 2nd mvt

Minuet in G WoO 10 No. 2

The Prisoners' Chorus from "Fidelio"

"Kyrie" from Missa Solemnis

Piano Quintet in Eb major: 2nd mvt

Index

Note: page numbers in **bold** are for main references to a person or place, e.g. the entry 'Augarten pavilion 66, 78–79, 81, **85**' shows there is most information about the Augarten pavilion on page 85

246

About the Authors

John Suchet, a regular presenter on Classic FM, remains one of the country's best-known television newscasters, having presented all of ITN's bulletins for nearly 20 years. Before becoming a newscaster John was a reporter for ITN, covering major events around the world. He has been honoured for both roles: Television Journalist of the Year 1986, and Television Newscaster of the Year 1996.

John retired from ITN in March 2004, but Channel Five television invited him back into the news studio in January 2006, and he now regularly presents Five News.

Away from the news, John's great passion is the life and work of Beethoven. He began writing the story of the great composer's life in 1990. It was published in three volumes entitled *The Last Master*, a trilogy which earned wide acclaim. The *Daily Telegraph* wrote:

This book is not for academics but for you and me and anyone moved by Beethoven's music, and will probably do more to further understanding of the composer than any professorial paper.

John now travels around the UK giving talks about Beethoven, *The Last Master*, accompanied by his own group of musicians. He has performed in more than 150 theatres, as well as Britain's major concert halls. He has also given his talk at an international symposium in Beethoven's home city, Vienna.

He regularly broadcasts both on television and radio about Beethoven's life and music. He was series consultant to the highly acclaimed 2005 BBC2 television series, 'The Genius of Beethoven'.

In 2000 John was appointed Honorary Doctor of Laws by his old university, the University of Dundee. In 2001 the Royal Academy of Music appointed him Honorary Fellow in recognition of his work on Beethoven, and in 2003 he was elected onto the Academy's governing body.

Darren Henley joined Classic FM in 1992, becoming Station Manager in 2004. He has written, edited or contributed to 13 books about classical music and musicians. He is the co-author of *The Classic FM Friendly Guide to Mozart*, also published by Hodder Arnold.

CLASSIC *f*M

The *Friendly* Guide to

Mozart

Darren Henley and Tim Lihoreau

Wolfgang Amadeus Mozart is arguably the greatest composer who ever lived. In the 250 years since his birth, the popularity of his music has soared and he is now recognized around the world as being at the top of the classical music tree.

The Classic FM *Friendly Guide to Mozart* takes you by the hand and provides you with a *friendly* introduction to the man and his music. In true Classic FM style we have removed the jargon that sometimes surrounds classical music to give you a fun, accessible read. Other *friendly* features are

- a CD with excerpts from Mozart's Top 20 hits, as voted for by listeners to the Classic FM 'Hall of Fame'
- a Mozart Mood Chart
- a list of Mozart's movie music.

The Classic FM *Friendly Guide to Mozart* tells you everything you ever wanted to know about Mozart and his music.

£9.99 ISBN 0 340 91395 9
EAN 978 0340 91395 6

CLASSIC *f*M

The *Friendly* Guide to

Music

Darren Henley

The Classic FM *Friendly Guide to Music* is the book
about classical music for people who wouldn't
normally consider buying a book on the subject,
but who are interested in developing a greater
understanding of classical music. It gives a friendly,
jargon-free overview of classical music from its
earliest times right through to the present day,
concentrating on the composers who are played
regularly on Classic FM.

The Classic FM *Friendly Guide to Music* takes you
on a journey through the five main eras of classical
music: early, baroque, classical, romantic and
contemporary. There are handy 'Instant Guides' to
each of the main composers featured in the book
and sections on

- music in films
- the Classic FM 'Hall of Fame'
- composers' quotes about each other

Other friendly features are

- a music timeline
- a music mood guide
- a CD with excerpts of the music so you can
  have a listen yourself

The Classic FM *Friendly Guide to Music* will help
you understand and enjoy the rich tapestry of
sounds, emotions and stories which go together to
make up classical music and its world.

£9.99 ISBN 0 340 94019 0
EAN 978 0340 94019 8